WILDSAM

Isle of sweet brooks of
      drinking-water—healthy air and soil!
Isle of the salty shore
      and breeze and brine!

—*Walt Whitman*

WILDSAM PURSUITS

*Places are endlessly complex: time, geography, culture and
happenings layered with millions of stories. And often, a place carries
a specific heritage, a definitive pursuit that people build their lives
around, a common trade, endeavor or natural resource that
might set the course for generations.*

For the East End of Long Island, this pursuit is farming.

Our sincere thanks to everyone whose insight and
recommendations helped us get to know the East End,
including Gaia Filicori, Layton Guenther, Jesse Joeckel, Pippa
Biddle, Tracey Minkin, Paul Brady, Peter Treiber Jr., Amanda
Merrow and Montauk Point Lighthouse historian Henry
Osmers. Special thanks to John v.H. Halsey, Yvette Salsedo
and the rest of the staff of the Peconic Land Trust for their help
and all the work they do. We look forward to sharing some
East End wine and farm-fresh meals with all of you soon.

WILDSAM FIELD GUIDES™

Published in the United States
by Wildsam Field Guides, Austin, Texas.

ISBN 978-1-4671-9970-4

Illustrations by Kaitlin Beebe

To find more field guides, please visit
www.wildsam.com

CONTENTS

Discover the people and places
that tell the story of Long Island's East End

WELCOME

WHEN YOU REACH the salt air and windswept beaches of eastern Long Island, the Peconic Bay splits the land in two. Together, these fingers of land form the East End; separately, they are the North Fork and South Fork. But here, bifurcation goes beyond the shape of the land: This is a place of dichotomies. A place of shingled cottages and modernist mansions. A place of fisherfolk and farmers, celebrities and financiers. Or maybe it's more true to say it's many places at once.

Conjuring glamour and Gatsbyesque parties, the phrase "the Hamptons"—by which many know the South Fork—is not often uttered by the people who live there. Geographic isolation and the weight of public perception have combined to stretch wide the gap between the place known to locals and the one most visitors see. That gap is perhaps smaller for the quieter North Fork, though it, too, is changing as more New Yorkers seek second homes here.

The stories in these pages go far beyond the seaside mansions and grandeur: Andrina Wekontash Smith explores the value of wampum and life on the Shinnecock Reservation. Bonnie Michelle Cannon sheds light on Bridgehampton's Black community. Marilee Foster's story of a family business adapting across generations reveals the history of the potato farms that once dominated the landscape.

How better to bridge the gap than to center the land itself, to touch its soil. Fertile ground [and the surrounding waters' bounty] made the East End fruitful and valuable long before the Long Island Rail Road or the Hampton Jitney traversed the island. For millennia, it sustained Indigenous peoples, including the Shinnecock, who shared their farming techniques with settlers.

Today, even as development has covered over much of that land, many farms remain. Painted roadside signs beckon: apples, tomatoes, local oysters. Some farms trace back a dozen generations. Some are the hard-won dreams of relative newcomers. Most are scrappy and small. These farms nurture residents and visitors alike, especially in summer, when time is measured by the ripening red of strawberries, the harvest of sweet corn, each savored bite a reminder that this is a place where the true richness goes deep into the ground. —The Editors

ESSENTIALS

*Trusted intel and traveler info about iconic culture,
geography and entry points to the East End's
traditions and institutions*

PLANNING

TRANSPORT

BUS

Hampton Jitney
NYC to eastern Long Island
hamptonjitney.com

....

TRAIN

Long Island Rail Road
Main & Montauk lines
lirr42.mta.info

LANDMARKS

OLD HOOK MILL

42 Main St, East Hampton
Stoutly smock-shaped, wood-shingled 1806 gristmill.

....

MONTAUK LIGHTHOUSE

2000 Montauk Hwy, Montauk
Looms over the South Fork's windblown easternmost point.

....

THE BIG DUCK

1012 Hwy 24, Flanders
Duck-shaped building dreamed up by a 1930s poultry farmer.

MEDIA

NEWSPAPER

The East Hampton Star
Weekly broadsheet owned by local Rattray family.

....

MAGAZINE

Dan's Papers
Dan Rattiner's quirky, free, large-format lifestyle mag.

CLIMATE

Out east, the surrounding waters keep weather pleasantly mild, extending the growing season far into fall. Cool breezes from the Long Island Sound and Atlantic Ocean provide a respite on warm, humid summer days. Winters are cold, but not as cold as elsewhere in the state. Sun is plentiful year-round; summer brings thunderstorms, while winters can be snowy. Hurricanes, though generally aimed farther south, do sometimes strike Long Island's vulnerable coastline, with damaging effects.

CALENDAR

FEB	Long Island Winterfest
MAR	Peak seal-watching season
APR	Cutchogue Rites of Spring concert series begins
MAY	Memorial Day heralds high season's start
JUN	Mattituck Strawberry Festival
JUL	Declaration of Independence reading in Orient
AUG	Artists & Writers Softball Game
SEP	Hampton Classic
OCT	Hamptons International Film Festival
NOV	East Hampton House & Garden Tour
DEC	Greenport Shellabration

GEOGRAPHY

Notable terrain formations and where to find them.

TERMINAL
MORAINE

A ridge of glacial
debris; two run the
length of Long
Island. *Montauk
Point State Park,
Montauk*

....

BAYMOUTH BAR

An accumulation
of sand, deposited
by waves, that cuts
off a bay from the
ocean, forming a
lagoon. *Mecox Bay,
Bridgehampton*

WALKING DUNES

U-shaped sand
mounds along the
coast, up to 80 feet
high; constantly
shifting. *Hither
Hills State Park,
Napeague*

....

KETTLE LAKES

Formed by ice
blocks left behind
after the ice sheet
retreated, later
filled by fresh
water. *Laurel Lake
Preserve, Laurel*

MARITIME
GRASSLANDS

Last remnants of
prairie that once
covered broad
swaths of the
Island. *Conscience
Point, Southampton*

....

TIDAL WETLANDS

Coastal areas of
vegetation subject
to the ocean's
tides are key to
flood protection.
*Napeague State
Park, Napeague*

TRADITIONS

A heritage deeply rooted in land and sea.

Potatoes	Farmed throughout the East End before real estate values took off in the 1980s. *Martin Sidor Farms, Mattituck*
Viticulture	Sandy, mineral-rich soils and a cool maritime climate have helped vineyards thrive in the last half-century. *Bedell Cellars, Cutchogue*
Aquaculture	Peconic Bay scallops, Blue Point oysters, Little Neck clams: shellfish bounty with an international reputation. *Little Creek Oyster Farm & Market, Greenport*
Surfing	Montauk's consistent beach breaks have attracted the cold-water dawn patrol for decades. *Ditch Plains, Montauk*
Homes	From shingled beach bungalows to rustic farmhouses to McMansions that would shock Jay Gatsby. *Preservation Long Island, Cold Spring Harbor*

FARM STANDS

A quick guide to favorite stops for farm-fresh goodness.

NORTH FORK	SOUTH FORK
LATHAM FARMS	**GREEN THUMB**
Orient	*Water Mill*
Nine generations, on the water	Produce and plants since 1961
DEEP ROOTS FARM	**AMBER WAVES FARM**
Southold	*Amagansett*
Self-serve eggs, chicken, produce	Cozy cafe, thriving CSA
TREIBER FARMS	**PIKE FARMS**
Peconic	*Sagaponack*
Father-son; sustainability focus	Produce, cut flowers, honey
SANG LEE FARMS	**BALSAM FARMS**
Peconic	*Amagansett*
Great organic greens and herbs	Over 100 tomato varieties
KK'S THE FARM	**ROUND SWAMP FARM**
Cutchogue	*East Hampton*
Biodynamic veg, sauces, pickles	One stop: seafood, fresh bread

CULTURAL INSTITUTIONS

PARRISH ART MUSEUM

279 Montauk Hwy, Water Mill

Exhibitions and programs celebrate the works of eastern Long Island artists inside a vast, modern barn amid 14 acres of meadow.

....

GUILD HALL

158 Main St, East Hampton

Multidisciplinary center includes a museum focused on Hamptons artists and a theater showcasing plays, dance, concerts and readings.

....

EAST END SEAPORT MUSEUM

103 3rd St, Greenport

Tells the story of Greenport's history as a whaling and shipbuilding port. Cruises to Long Beach Bar "Bug" Lighthouse begin here.

SCENIC DRIVES
AND PUBLIC LANDS

Notable natural sites and paths worth taking throughout the East End.

HALLOCK STATE PARK PRESERVE
A serene stretch of shorefront. Short trails through the woods and nearly a mile of pristine beach along the glittering Long Island Sound. *Riverhead*

....

NORTH FORK TRAIL SCENIC BYWAY
This 13-mile drive wends through the hamlets of the North Fork, with plenty of wineries and farm stands to stop at along the way. *Southold to Orient Point*

....

ELIZABETH A. MORTON NATIONAL WILDLIFE REFUGE
Nature trails pass through lush and diverse habitats, including grasslands and a salt marsh lagoon. Look out for piping plovers, a threatened species. *Noyack*

....

ORIENT BEACH STATE PARK
Out at the North Fork's farthest reach, the beach along Gardiners Bay features rare maritime red cedar forest. Osprey, herons and egrets are among the park's regulars. *Orient*

....

NASSAU POINT ROAD
A causeway connects the quiet Nassau Point peninsula to the North Fork mainland. Gorgeous sunset drive, with Peconic Bay views all the way. *Cutchogue*

....

MONTAUK POINT STATE PARK
Trails, surfing and surf fishing at the South Fork's rugged eastern tip. Home of the state's oldest lighthouse. Watch for seals on the rocks. *Montauk*

....

PAUMANOK PATH
Wander among dunes and kettle ponds, beech forests and marshlands via this connected series of hiking trails extending 125 miles. *Rocky Point to Montauk Point*

MEDIA

FILM

Eternal Sunshine of the Spotless Mind

The Great Gatsby

Pollock

Grey Gardens

Something's Gotta Give

Inside Job

Jaws

Weekend at Bernie's

The Bonfire of the Vanities

Blue Jasmine

MUSIC

Billy Joel
Storm Front

Rufus Wainwright
"Montauk"

De La Soul
"Long Island Degrees"

The Rolling Stones
"Memory Motel"

Mindy Smith
Long Island Shores

BOOKS

↦ *Men's Lives: The Surfmen and Baymen of the South Fork* by Peter Matthiessen: The writer and naturalist's elegy to the fisherfolk of the East End and their disappearing way of life.

↦ *Hamptons Bohemia: Two Centuries of Artists and Writers on the Beach* by Helen A. Harrison and Constance Ayers Denne: Tracing the arts on the South Fork; Winslow Homer to Jackson Pollock, Whitman to Steinbeck.

↦ *Sag Harbor* by Colson Whitehead: Benji, a nerdy Black teenager from Manhattan, chronicles the ebb and flow of summer life in 1985.

↦ *The Lost Boys of Montauk* by Amanda M. Fairbanks: We'll never know what happened to the *Wind Blown*, a fishing boat that disappeared in 1984. But Fairbanks has painstakingly rendered the details of the four lives lost.

↦ *The Vineyard: The Pleasures and Perils of Creating an American Family Winery* by Louisa Hargrave: The story of the North Fork's first commercial winery began with the purchase of an old potato farm in 1973.

↦ *Leave the World Behind* by Rumaan Alam: A family's Hamptons idyll is interrupted when their AirBnB's owners show up amid a region-wide blackout. A dryly funny dystopian thriller.

ISSUES

Housing prices	Pandemic demand sent already high prices soaring in the tony Hamptons—and on the less-expensive North Fork too. Service workers, who already struggle to find affordable housing, are increasingly priced out of the communities where they work. **EXPERT:** *Bonnie Michelle Cannon, chair, Southampton Housing Authority*
Coastal erosion	Due in part to the increasing frequency of severe storms like 2012's Superstorm Sandy, both the North Shore and South Shore of eastern Long Island lose ground each year to erosion. **EXPERT:** *Henry J. Bokuniewicz, professor, Stony Brook University School of Marine and Atmospheric Sciences*
Water quality	As New Yorkers fled to the centralized-sanitation-lacking Hamptons amid the COVID-19 pandemic, older septic systems were overrun, causing nasty backups and sending nitrogen leaking into surrounding waterways. Suffolk County drinking water has high nitrate levels to begin with. **EXPERT:** *Peter Topping, executive director, Peconic Baykeeper*
Helicopter noise	In recent years, some deep-pocketed New Yorkers have opted to skip the traffic and zip to eastern Long Island in helicopters, resulting in so much noise that locals have pushed for the East Hampton Airport to shut down. **EXPERT:** *Kathleen Cunningham, chairwoman, Quiet Skies Coalition*

STATISTICS

89% .... Suffolk County farms that were family-owned in 2017
$1.695 million .... Median price of a Hamptons home in 2020
69 .... Wineries in Suffolk County in 2019
2.5 ..... Hours from Manhattan to East Hampton on the Hampton Jitney
8 .... Minutes from Greenport to Shelter Island by ferry
30 .... Weight in tons of The Big Duck in Flanders

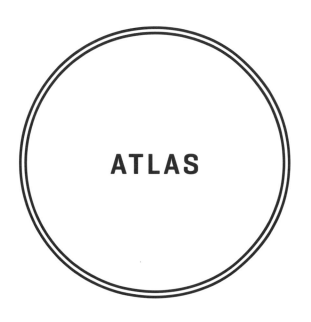

ATLAS

A guide to eastern Long Island's communities and
landscapes, including curated favorites, towns and hamlets,
and a revelatory road trip

BESTS

FOOD & DRINK

ROADSIDE CAFE

Estia's Little Kitchen

1615 Sag Harbor Tpke Sag Harbor

A gem in the woods. Try chilaquiles for lunch, paella "mono pot" for dinner.

....

OYSTERS

Little Creek Oyster Farm

37 Front St Greenport

So fresh you can shuck your own for half price.

....

BURGERS

LT Burger

62 Main St Sag Harbor

Classic joint. The topping-heaped milkshakes taste as good as they look in a tall glass.

NEW AMERICAN

North Fork Table & Inn

57225 Main Rd Southold

Field and sea define Michelin-starred chef John Fraser's ever-evolving menu.

....

BREAKFAST

The Hampton Maid

259 E Montauk Hwy Hampton Bays

Douse pancakes with syrup and creamery butter; enjoy Shinnecock Bay views.

....

BISTRO

Almond

1 Ocean Rd Bridgehampton

Tin ceilings, friendly vibes, chefs who call the nearby growers and baymen friends, 20 years running.

INSTITUTION

Nick & Toni's

136 N Main St East Hampton

Italian-meets-Mediterranean fare and people-watching have both earned their rep here.

....

HISTORIC

The 1770 House

143 Main St, East Hampton

Delicately prepared local seafood amid antiques in the heart of downtown.

....

SUNDAY SUPPER

Vine Street Café

41 S Ferry Rd Shelter Island

Cozy cottage where the bolognese is Ina Garten-approved and the bouillabaisse is legend.

TASTING MENU
18 Bay
23 N Ferry Rd
Shelter Island
Elegantly plated
antipasti and hand-
made pastas. House
dates to 1873.

....

SEAFOOD SHACK
The Lobster Roll
1980 Montauk Hwy
Amagansett
Iconic "LUNCH"
sign beckons; name-
sake roll delivers.

....

RAW BAR
The Bell & Anchor
3253 Noyac Rd
Sag Harbor
Snag a bar seat,
plenty of oysters and
little necks, and a
zippy cocktail.

....

TACOS
Lucharitos
119 Main St
Greenport
Guac [with lobster!]
is extra, but worth it.

....

ICE CREAM
Snowflake
1148 W Main St
Riverhead
Retro scoop shop.
Homemade seasonal
fruit toppings.

WEEKEND BRUNCH
Bruce & Son
208 Main St
Greenport
Family-owned spot
with a rustic feel and
festive dishes.

....

SUSHI
Sen
23 Main St
Sag Harbor
Chefs transform
tuna and clams into
extraordinary dishes.

....

NEIGHBORHOOD CAFE
Love Lane Kitchen
240 Love Ln
Mattituck
Homey goodness.
Save room for the
coconut cake.

....

NO B.S.
The Dock
482 W Lake Dr
Montauk
Just cold beer, hot
chowder and fisher-
men's stories.

....

SUNSET SPOT
Bostwick's on
the Harbor
39 Gann Rd
East Hampton
Three Mile Harbor
looks good with
mussels and a drink.

COCKTAILS
Brix & Rye
308 Main St
Greenport
Cozy, below-street-
level haunt.

....

BREWERY
North Fork Brewing
24 E 2nd St
Riverhead
Sip IPAs made with
the brewery's own
Peconic-grown hops.

....

DIVE BAR
Liar's Saloon
401 W Lake Dr
Montauk
How big was that
fish? Won't matter
after your second
chocolate mudslide.

....

WINE TASTING
Corey Creek Tap
Room
45470 Main Rd
Southold
Innovative wines on
tap from the Bedell
Cellars team.

....

WINERY
Macari Vineyards
150 Bergen Ave
Mattituck
Stellar sustainably
made wines; views of
the gorgeous estate.

LODGING

HISTORIC
The Maidstone
East Hampton
themaidstone.com
Storied Greek revival
buildings eclectically
restored with Scandi-
navian flare.

....

OCEANSIDE
Gurney's Montauk
Resort
Montauk
gurneysresorts.com
Crashing waves,
ocean-fed pool and
airy living spaces.

....

MARINA CLASSIC
Baron's Cove
Sag Harbor
caperesorts.com
Nautically oriented
rooms, marina views
to channel your
inner sea captain.

....

LUXURY
Topping Rose House
Bridgehampton
toppingrosehouse.com
19th-century man-
sion with a Jean
Georges restaurant.

ON THE SOUND
Sound View
Greenport
Greenport
soundviewgreenport.com
Roadside [and beach-
side] motel revived
with rustic glamor.

....

BUNGALOW
A Room at the Beach
Bridgehampton
iwantaroomat
thebeach.com
Walk among the
redwoods and relax
in the cedar sauna.

....

BEACH HAVEN
Marram
Montauk
marrammontauk.com
Artfully minimalist
spaces. Drift off to
the shush of the sea.

....

BED & BREAKFAST
Cedar House
on Sound
Mattituck
cedarhouseonsound.com
Cleverly converted
potato barn; on-
property vineyard.

SPA RETREAT
Shou Sugi
Ban House
Water Mill
shousugibanhouse.com
Secluded wellness
sanctuary. Yoga,
massage, hydro-
therapy and more

....

HARBORSIDE INN
The Chequit
Shelter Island Heights
thechequithotel.com
Pastries on the
porch, epic sunsets
on the bay.

....

BOUTIQUE
Lin Beach House
Greenport
linbeachhouse.com
Tranquil, light-filled.
Sample Matchbook
Distilling Co.'s wares
at the on-site bar.

....

IN-TOWN
The Roundtree
Amagansett
theroundtreehotels.com
Low-key luxury. Ride
a beach cruiser to
town or the shore.

BEACH HIKE
Napeague State Park
Amagansett
parks.ny.gov
Take the Promised
Land Trail, a mellow
2-mile jaunt from
pines to sand.

....

BIKE RENTAL
Rotations
Southampton
rotationsbicyclecenter.
com
On two wheels, you
won't miss a thing
[except the traffic].

....

CAMPING
Hither Hills
Campground
Montauk
reserveamerica.com
Nothing beats sleep-
ing by the beach.
Reserve ahead.

....

BIRD WATCHING
Phillips Pond
Preserve
Southampton
peconiclandtrust.org
Songbird tunes
among the dunes.

LIGHTHOUSE
Montauk
Lighthouse
Montauk
montauklighthouse.com
Climb up and take in
The End from the
top of the tower.

....

SURF LESSONS
Hamptons Surf Co.
Southampton
hamptonssurf.co
Let pros Kurt Rist
and Asaya Brusa
guide you into the
swells at surf camp
or private lessons.

....

OCEAN BEACH
Cooper's Beach
Southampton
The parking fee pays
for itself in views of
historic mansions
and the Atlantic.

....

BAY BEACH
Hay Beach
Shelter Island
Panoramic views of
glittering Gardiners
Bay at one of few
dog-friendly beaches.

BOAT RENTAL
Pontoon Paddler
Westhampton Beach
pontoonpaddler.com
Pack a cooler, bring
friends and leave the
rest to Captain Tony.

....

HORSEBACK RIDE
Deep Hollow Ranch
Montauk
deephollowranch.org
Canter along the
Long Island Sound
at the oldest working
ranch in the country.

....

FOLKLORE
Camp Hero
State Park
Montauk
parks.ny.gov
Fishing-village-cum-
Air-Force-base, plus
the *Stranger Things*
origin story.

....

LAVENDER FIELD
Lavender by the Bay
East Marion
lavenderbythebay.com
A sea of lavender
that blooms three
times each year.

SHOPS

See page 110 for a shopping and lodging directory.

GENERAL STORE

Orient Country Store

950 Village Ln
Orient

Historic spot's new owners have maintained all the charm. Excellent pastries and egg sandwiches.

....

GOURMET MARKET

Hen of the Woods Market

48 Hampton Rd
Southampton

Hard-to-find specialty items for elegant cooking.

....

FURNITURE

Hildreth's Home Goods

51 Main St
Southampton

1842 opening makes it the oldest continuously family-run store in the U.S.

TREASURES

LUMBER+Salt

5570 Sound Ave
Jamesport

Endlessly wanderable salvage and esoterica, from fireplace mantles to stained glass windows.

....

VINTAGE

The Times Vintage

429 Main St
Greenport

Floral-print dresses, eclectic decor, vinyl and appropriately funky vibes.

....

DESIGNER GOODS

Tiina the Store

216 Main St
Amagansett

Finnish-born stylist Tiina Laakkonen fills a 19th-century building with her favorite things.

SLIPPERS

Sabah House

137 Main St
Amagansett

Stylish, adaptable handmade leather unisex slippers so soft, you'll want a pair in every shade.

....

SURF SHOP

Air + Speed

795 Montauk Hwy
Montauk

Stu and Catherine have everything you need for a day of Ditch Plains shredding.

....

AMERICANA

Double RL

57 Main St
East Hampton

Classic workwear-inspired designs. Named for Ralph and Ricky's Colorado ranch.

FLORIST

Bridgehampton
Florist
2400 Montauk Hwy
Bridgehampton
Barefoot Contessa
appearances and
bold blossoms.

....

MARINE SUPPLY

Preston's Chandlery
102 Main St
Greenport
Family-owned since
it first filled shipyard
needs in the 1880s.

....

ANTIQUES

North Found & Co.
2845 Peconic Ln
Peconic
Hadley Wiggins-
Marin's collection of
backstock treasures.

....

BOUTIQUE

Joey Wölffer
11 Madison St
Sag Harbor
Luxe clothes and
jewelry from stylish
entrepreneur Joey.

....

ART SUPPLY

Golden Eagle Art
144 N Main St
East Hampton
Pro-level arts em-
porium, plus local
crafts for sale.

MODERN DECOR

touchGOODS
53740 Main Rd
Southold
Orange retro lamps,
snazzy antique brass
and copper sconces.

....

KITCHENWARE

Loaves & Fishes
Cookshop
2266 Montauk Hwy
Bridgehampton
From the family be-
hind the long-run-
ning gourmet shop.

....

HOME GOODS

E-E Home
140 Main St
Amagansett
Gorgeous tabletop
goods, Japanese
gardening tools.

....

BAIT & TACKLE

Tight Lines Tackle
53 Bay St
Sag Harbor
Jam-packed for surf-
casters and charter
captains alike.

....

JEWELRY

Love Adorned
156 Main St
Amagansett
Fine pieces from
tiger's eye rings to
gold skull earrings.

WOMEN'S CLOTHING

Kirna Zabête
66 Newtown Ln
East Hampton
Vibrant, high-fashion
edit just off Main St.

....

GARDEN

Marders
120 Snake Hollow Rd
Bridgehampton
World of green in a
19th-century barn.

....

WINE & SPIRITS

Bogey's
Bottled Goods
54655 Route 25
Southold
Neighborhood gem.
Local, global picks.

....

BOOKSTORES

Canio's *Sag Harbor*
BookHampton
East Hampton
Southampton Books
Southampton
Sag Harbor Books
Sag Harbor
Harper's Books
East Hampton
Burton's Bookstore
Greenport
Black Cat Books
Shelter Island
Finley's Fiction
Shelter Island Heights
Red Jacket Books
Westhampton Beach

ART & CRAFT

ANNUAL SHOW
Springs Invitational
Art Show
East Hampton
ashawagh-hall.org
Dates back to the
abstract expression-
ists drawn to Springs
in the 1960s.

....

FAIR
Art Market
Bridgehampton
artmarkethamptons.com
Weekend of modern
art from 90 galleries.

....

ARTS LAB
The Watermill
Center
Water Mill
watermillcenter.org
Theater director and
artist Robert Wilson
founded this haven
for emerging artists.

....

MULTIMEDIA ARTIST
Scott Bluedorn
East Hampton
scottbluedorn.com
Detailed, nautically
inspired drawings.
Collage, prints too.

BIPOC ART
Ma's House
Southampton
mashouse.studio
Communal space
run by Shinnecock
artist Jeremy Den-
nis. Artist studio,
library and more.

....

GALLERY
VSOP Projects
Greenport
vsopprojects.com
A vibrant North
Fork hub for con-
temporary art.

....

RESIDENCY
The Church
Sag Harbor
thechurchsagharbor.org
Founded by April
Gornik and Eric
Fischl. No religion
here but creativity.

....

MURALIST
Kara Hoblin
Greenport
karahoblin.com
Known across the
North Fork for her
whimsical chalk art.

ARTS CENTER
The Arts Center at
Duck Creek
East Hampton
duckcreekarts.org
Exhibitions and con-
certs at a restored
19th-century barn.

....

WOODWORKING
Michael Javidi
Greenport
michaeljavidi.com
Shipwright experi-
ence influences his
elegantly curved
hanging chairs.

....

ART EDUCATION
The Art Barge
Napeague
damico-art.org
World War II Navy
barge reinvented as a
beached class space.

....

PAINTER
Whitney B. Hansen
Sag Harbor
whitneybhansen.com
Dreamy scenes
combine woodcut
techniques and hand-
painting in oils.

EXPERTS

BOATBUILDING

Wooden Boatworks

woodenboatworks.com

Follow the fragance of wood shavings and pine tar to Hanff's Boatyard.

....

CONSERVATION

Seatuck Environmental Association

seatuck.org

Protecting open spaces, waterways and key species like horseshoe crabs and river otters.

....

HOSPITALITY

Mark Smith

@smarky1

Co-founder of Honest Man, restaurant group behind Nick & Toni's, Coche Comedor and more.

....

BAKING

Kathleen King

tatesbakeshop.com

Created the iconic buttery, crisp, thin, crunchy perfection of Tate's cookies.

COOKBOOKS

Ina Garten

barefootcontessa.com

The effortless entertaining queen loves to champion local shops, eateries and farms.

....

VITICULTURE

Rich Olsen-Harbich

bedellcellars.com

Bedell Cellars' winemaker's roots go deep: he literally wrote the North Fork's AVA application in 1986.

....

ECOLOGY

Carl Safina

carlsafina.org

Award-winning writing explores humans' connection to other living things.

....

FUN

Whalebone

whalebonemag.com

Hand-printed T-shirts, a playful magazine and other Montauk-rooted dabblings.

BLACK HISTORY

Plain Sight Project

plainsightproject.org

The mission: to identify enslaved persons who lived in East Hampton and gather their stories.

....

INDIGENOUS RIGHTS

Tela Troge

@telatroge

Shinnecock attorney and activist fights for tribal sovereignty.

....

HAMPTONIANA

Dan Rattiner

danspapers.com

Prolific writer, longtime editor of *Dan's Papers* and propagator of the occasional hoax.

....

INDIGENOUS HISTORY

Jeremy Dennis

jeremynative.com

Photographic project On This Site documents significant Native American sites via an interactive map.

CITIES & TOWNS

Though most are technically villages and hamlets, the communities of the East End possess personalities as bold and distinct as any city's.

SOUTHOLD

All along County Road 48, signs for the area's vineyards beckon—a notable attraction indeed, but not the only one. And all that wine pairs well with the bounty of the North Fork's rich farmlands and fresh seafood, on full display in the hamlet of Southold. At ABOUT FOOD, proprietor Gerard Lane offers local honeys, jams and mustards along with his own recipes. Whatever you choose, you'll find wares on which to serve it just a few doors down amid the vintage treasures at WHITE FLOWER FARMHOUSE. Pick up whatever's freshly caught at SOUTHOLD FISH MARKET or dine out at NORTH FORK TABLE & INN, where nearly everything comes straight from field or sea. Saturday nights at the CUSTER INSTITUTE & OBSERVATORY, Long Island's oldest public observatory, feature guided views of the sky.

PARK STOP	POPULATION: 5,904
Goldsmith's Inlet	COFFEE: North Fork Roasting Co.
Hike up a bluff, along dunes	BEST DAY OF THE YEAR:
and down to a quiet beach.	Candlelight Tour, November

GREENPORT

Spinning past the downtown shops and the boats of the Greenport Harbor on a century-old carousel, it may feel as though time stands still in this one-time whaling and shipbuilding hub. But, though old, the carousel has only stood here since 1995, and since then, Greenport has kept right on changing as a real estate boom has brought more and more city folk seeking second homes. Restaurants like 1943 PIZZA BAR [the clams casino pie is a must], Robby Beaver's Frisky Oyster with its decadent red interior, and seasonally minded NOAH'S have fueled the village's growing vitality. For a nightcap, head to Brix & Rye for an inventive take on a classic drink, or go fully classic at historic CLAUDIO'S before bedding down at the SILVER SANDS MOTEL, where wood paneling keeps the '50s feel alive.

BREW STOP	POPULATION: 2,264
Greenport Harbor	COFFEE: Aldo's Coffee Company
Brewing Company	BEST DAY OF THE YEAR:
Tasty ales in a former firehouse.	Maritime Festival, September

MATTITUCK

Named for the Algonquian term for "great creek," this small hamlet within the town of Southold abuts the Long Island Sound. A day in Mattituck should begin with wine tasting. Kick things off at the 500-acre MACARI VINEYARDS, home to red, white, sparkling and rosé. The crown-capped, bubbly pink Horses is a winning pick. ROSE HILL VINEYARDS & INN features a comfortable tasting room and diverse wines. Downtown, you'll find Love Lane, a tiny but charming stretch of shops including The Village Cheese Shop, Lombardi's Love Lane Market and the petite LOVE LANE KITCHEN — which is where you want to be come dinnertime. Local wines and produce inform the seasonally driven menu; save room for homemade desserts, like a towering slice of coconut cake with coconut icing.

PIZZA STOP	POPULATION: 4,676
Pizza Rita	COFFEE: North Fork Doughnut Company
Chewy Neapolitan pies, charred to perfection.	BEST DAY OF THE YEAR: Mattituck Strawberry Festival, June

CUTCHOGUE

No matter the season, a trip to Cutchogue is best spent outdoors. At 8 HANDS FARM, sheep and chickens mill about the land while, inside, guests are greeted with a stocked nose-to-tail butcher, fresh produce and eggs, and irresistibly flaky pastries straight from the oven—ideal fuel for an early hike at the neighboring DOWNS FARM PRESERVE, where the salt air somehow stays crisp even on the warmest summer days. Family-operated vineyards SUHRU [founded by renowned Australian winemaker Russell Hearn and his wife Susan] and LIEB CELLARS [where Mark Lieb bottled his first wine in 1993 under Hearn's tutelage] capture this weather—and feeling—in glasses of herbaceous rieslings and pinot blancs and fruit-forward merlots.

ART STOP	POPULATION: 3,200
Alex Ferrone Gallery	COFFEE: Karen's Country Delicatessen
A range of photo-based works, plus paintings and sculptures.	BEST DAY OF THE YEAR: Cutchogue Lions Car Show, October

MONTAUK

Spanning 13 miles along the South Fork's farthest reach, Montauk is known as "The End" for good reason—and when you're out there, you can feel it. The longer haul from New York City [and everywhere else] and excellent surf have bred a laid-back vibe and kept locals rooted and loyal. In summer, you can't go wrong with the decade-old CROW'S NEST hotel and restaurant. In the colder months, business slows down, but the larger-than-life dishes at HARVEST ON FORT POND [try the marinated lamb ribs] warm spirits year-round. On balmier nights, grab a burger from JOHN'S DRIVE-IN, which has served up flat-top-style patties since 1967, and head over to DITCH PLAINS for a chance to watch surfers catch swells.

SUNSET SPOT	POPULATION: 3,685
The Montauket	COFFEE: Bluestone Lane
Sip a beer as oranges and pinks fill bay and sky.	BEST DAY OF THE YEAR: When the first hurricane hits [waves!]

EAST HAMPTON

Famous for its pristine ocean, bay beaches and sprawling celebrity homes, East Hampton runs 25 miles to the South Fork's easternmost point. A de rigueur day starts with breakfast at the light-filled, James Beard Award-winning CARISSA'S THE BAKERY [don't skip the olive ciabatta]. Next: a stroll among the sculptures at LONGHOUSE RESERVE, a trip back to the 17th century at MULFORD FARM or world-class shopping in the village. Have a harborside Italian dinner at the recently expanded MOBY'S, or go for farm-fresh fare [and quite possibly star sightings] at Nick & Toni's. In lieu of a nightcap, catch the sunset at MAIDSTONE PARK BEACH, a slip of sand on the spectacular west-facing Three Mile Harbor, before turning in at the historic and elegant 1770 HOUSE.

MARTINI SPOT	POPULATION: 28,385
East Hampton Grill	COFFEE: Hello Oma
Ample pour, blue-cheese-stuffed olives optional.	BEST DAY OF THE YEAR: Tumbleweed Tuesday, September

SAG HARBOR

Benches and picnic tables line the shore along Sag Harbor, overlooking the cove and bay—an idyllic spot to sit [preferably while sharing one of ESPRESSO DA ASPORTO's famed focaccia sandwiches with a friend] and let the mind wander back to the 1800s, when the sleepy village's main industry was whaling. Your imagination doesn't have to tread too far, though, with the SAG HARBOR WHALING MUSEUM a 10-minute walk down Main Street. Farther on, step into the stacks of CANIO'S BOOKS, overflowing with novels from locals, like Colson Whitehead, and used texts of all kinds. The past is also present in the wide-ranging inventory of SAGE STREET ANTIQUES [weekends only], and in the harbor-side rooms at Baron's Cove, where John Steinbeck and Truman Capote were once regulars.

FILM STOP	POPULATION: 2,283
Sag Harbor Cinema	COFFEE: Grindstone Coffee & Donuts
Arthouse restored after a major fire. FYI: Great croissants.	BEST DAY OF THE YEAR: HarborFest, September

BRIDGEHAMPTON

Before the area east of Sagg Pond was renamed for a bridge built in 1686, settlers called it Bullhead. The Shinnecock knew it as Mecox, and Sagaponack before that. Today, Bridgehampton is home to The Hampton Classic Horse Show, a thriving restaurant scene and some of the Hamptons' priciest real estate. At 20-year-old ALMOND, bistro classics take on a local bent, like steak frites showcasing Sagaponack-grown potatoes. Newcomer ARMIN & JUDY offers everything from breakfast-centric baked goods to sit-down dinners [and compelling pizzas, to boot]. For all the hamlet's high-profile bustle, its most special spot is a quieter one: BRIDGE GARDENS. The 5-acre botanical garden maintained by the Peconic Land Trust includes sculpture, native and non-native species, and a vegetable garden that supports a local food pantry.

BRUNCH STOP	POPULATION: 1,323
Bobby Van's	COFFEE: L & W Market
A 14-ounce sirloin; thin, crispy fries. One of the Hamptons' best deals.	BEST DAY OF THE YEAR: Trick-or-treating, October

SOUTHAMPTON

The Shinnecock Indian Nation has long been the heart of Southampton. Their tribal name, "People of the Stony Shore," is an apt one for this community of fishermen and farmers, which you can explore on the water with a guided TUKTU PADDLE TOUR, featuring Indigenous culture, plants and a sampling of shellfish, and on land at the SOUTHAMPTON ARTS CENTER. Shinnecock contributions to local culture are not a thing of the past; rather, they're celebrated at institutions like MA'S HOUSE & BIPOC ART STUDIO, which hosts community events and tours. Sating your appetite on the reservation is the SHINNECOCK LOBSTER FACTORY, open daily for locally caught seafood. No Southampton visit is complete without a trip to Cooper's Beach, cruising by the grand estates of Gin Lane along the way.

DOUGHNUT STOP	POPULATION: 3,328
Ye Olde Bake Shoppe	COFFEE: Raindrop's Cafe
Can't-miss jelly-filled confections. Cash only.	BEST DAY OF THE YEAR: Shinnecock Powwow, September

WESTHAMPTON BEACH

As its name suggests, Westhampton Beach lies west of the "other" Hamptons—20 miles west, to be exact, before the South Fork splits from the North. But its oceanfront beauty is no less remarkable. Hundred-year-old ECKART'S LUNCHEONETTE continues to offer old-fashioned soda fountain ambience and a menu of classic, comforting breakfast and lunch dishes. Follow the locals from their stools to HASKELL'S OUTPOST, where you can get outfitted with fresh bait and sturdy gear for a day of luring in bluefish and flounder on Quantuck Bay. Looking for live music, comedy shows, dance performances or film screenings? See what's on the calendar at the WESTHAMPTON BEACH PERFORMING ARTS CENTER, a year-round fixture for community-driven entertainment after a quiet day by the water.

SUNSET STOP	POPULATION: 1,791 COFFEE: Caffeine
John Scott's Surf Shack	BEST DAY OF THE YEAR:
Snag a patio seat to watch the sun set over Moriches Bay.	Westhampton Beach Festival of the Arts, September

ROAD TRIP

*The ideal East End adventure starts at the South Fork's beaches and
ends on the North Fork with wine aplenty and farm-fresh goodness.*

CHOOSE YOUR BEACH

Take your pick from among the best South Fork beaches that are open to nonresidents.

An inconvenient but important truth: Many East End beaches—especially the dramatic South Shore spots, with their slouching sandy bluffs and strong Atlantic surf—are open only to residents. But there are also beautiful beaches where visitors can pay to park. You just have to know where to go. [Rather not pay? Ditch the car; beaches like Georgica and Indian Wells are easily accessed by bike or foot.]

FOSTER MEMORIAL BEACH, SAG HARBOR

The locals call this Long Beach, and it is long indeed—about a mile from end to end. You'll want to stay for a sweeping sunset over the bay. Unlike many Hamptons beaches, Long Beach allows you to buy a day pass at the tollbooth. *Lunch rec: lobster rolls from Harbor Market and Kitchen.*

....

SAGG MAIN BEACH, SAGAPONACK

Behind some of the area's grandest estates lies one of the most desirable places to hang out on a summer afternoon, especially if you favor a gentle surf break. *Lunch rec: pulled pork sandwiches and whoopie pies at TownLine BBQ.*

....

MECOX BEACH, BRIDGEHAMPTON

One of the most beautiful and serene spots of sand in the Hamptons. *Lunch rec: a picnic of whatever's fresh at the Milk Pail.*

....

ATLANTIC AVENUE BEACH, AMAGANSETT

The surf can be heavy here, which is why you'll see lots of guards. But the beach is worth it: miles of sand, a great view and an epic Hamptons scene. On weekdays, out-of-towners can pay $50 to get in. *Lunch rec: fresh focaccia and fish at il Buco al Mare.*

....

KIRK PARK BEACH, MONTAUK

Ten years ago, there was little to no competition at this beach, which still offers parking for nonresidents, even on the weekends [for a price]. Arrive early enough to secure a spot and beat the crowds, and you'll be rewarded with an achingly beautiful view, soft sand and—if you're lucky—a pod of playful whales spouting offshore. *Lunch rec: flat-top-seared burgers at John's Drive-In.*

SOUTH FORK ART-HOPPING

<table>
<tr><td>DAY
2</td><td>SOUTH FORK ART-HOPPING
The East End's landscape and quiet have long drawn artists, so it's no surprise that the area hosts a rich array of art institutions.</td></tr>
</table>

Start at the **PARRISH ART MUSEUM**—the long, barn-inspired building is itself a work of art. Rotating exhibitions showcase an impressive range of pieces by Long Island-rooted artists; the museum holds the largest public collection of impressionist William Merritt Chase. Break for lunch in Amagansett [tortas at **LA FONDITA** or dosas at **HAMPTON CHUTNEY CO.**] before heading up to the **POLLOCK-KRASNER HOUSE**, where a walk through the abstract expressionists' home and studio provides an intimate glimpse of the lives behind the works. While you're in Springs, stop by the **THE SPRINGS TAVERN**, known as Jungle Pete's in the days when Pollock and Willem de Kooning bent their elbows there. Or keep the creative mood going at **CHANNING DAUGHTERS WINERY**, where weird and wild sculptures by Walter Channing [father of the eponymous daughters] pepper the grounds and winemaker Christopher Tracy crafts a killer pét-nat.

DAY 3

EXPLORING SHELTER ISLAND
```
Tucked between the two forks, this small, quiet
island is well worth the ferry ride.
```

HIKE *Mashomack Coastal Preserve*

At this 2,350-acre preserve, walking trails meander among forests and creeks. Start your day with the easy, accessible Joan C. Coles Trail, or tackle the 3.4-mile Green Trail.

SWIM *Wades Beach*

Shelter Island is home to a number of pristine bay beaches. At Wades Beach, gentle waves and warm water beckon—though do bring a beach chair. The sand is a rocky, shelly mix.

LUNCH *Marie Eiffel Market*

Cafe or market, no bad choices: Marie Eiffel's breads and pastries are legendary on Shelter Island, though her market also serves sandwiches, burgers, pastas and more.

FARM VISIT *Sylvester Manor Educational Farm*

Learn about what's native to Shelter Island, and what produce grows here. Stop at the farm stand to see what's local and fresh.

SUNSET SPOT *Crescent Beach*

Many call it Sunset Beach, for the event and for the hotel and restaurant that bear that name. Time it right to watch the orange orb fall into the bay, cocktail in hand.

DINNER *18 Bay*

Reserve your table in advance and enjoy the Italian-inspired culinary stylings of Elizabeth Ronzetti and Adam Kopels across a locally inflected multicourse meal.

> *Sylvester Manor began as a plantation. Today, it is a sustainable farm, and its stewards seek to preserve and share its history. Curator and archivist Donnamarie Barnes works to tell the stories of the enslaved and Indigenous peoples of this place; check the manor's website to keep up with events and exhibitions. sylvestermanor.org*

NORTH FORK WINE-TASTING TOUR

With diverse grapes, wine styles and tasting experiences, Long Island wine country has something for every palate.

More than three dozen tasting rooms dot the two primary roads that stretch roughly 30 miles from Riverhead to Orient Point.

SPARKLING POINTE *Southold*

The area's only strictly-sparkling winery makes classically styled wines from the grapes of Champagne, as well as some creative takes. Pops of color—artwork, geodes—decorate the Brazilian Carnaval-inspired tasting room.

CROTEAUX VINEYARDS *Southold*

Another specialty winery: here, it's rosé all day—sparkling and still, mostly from merlot clones, but also cabernet franc. Step into the small tasting room, which opens onto a garden surrounded by historic barns, and you'll swear you've been transported to the French countryside.

LENZ WINERY *Peconic*

At Lenz, the tasting barn and courtyard are as classic as the wines. Local standards merlot and chardonnay dominate, but winemaker Thomas Spotteck also crafts outstanding sparkling wine and the rare, delicious East End cabernet sauvignon.

MACARI VINEYARDS *Mattituck*

The Macari family's twin emphases on sustainability and hospitality—including tastings in private glamping tents—are reason enough to visit. The wines are also among the region's best, and don't skip the cheese and charcuterie.

PAUMANOK VINEYARDS

Aquebogue

On top of excellent examples of cabernet franc, chardonnay, sauvignon blanc, merlot and petit verdot, second-generation winemaker Kareem Massoud also makes the area's best rieslings and a chenin blanc with a near cult-like following.

BEDELL CELLARS *Cutchogue*

Veteran winemaker Rich Olsen-Harbich's wide-ranging portfolio includes the local stars [merlot, cabernet franc, chardonnay, sauvignon blanc] along with less common grapes like malbec and viognier—but made using ambient yeasts and less new oak than most.

COVID-era changes: Reservations and sit-down, restaurant-style tastings are more common, and many wineries offer food menus too.

FARM-FRESH BOUNTY

Take in a sampling of the North Fork's vast
array of farm stands and farmlands.

Small farms old and new dot the North Fork, from U-pick fields to farm stands galore, many of them within a potato's throw of the hamlet of Southold. Get the lay of the land, and maybe learn a thing or two, at the **AGRICULTURAL CENTER AT CHARNEWS FARM**, one of the Peconic Land Trust's stewardship hubs. The grounds are open to the public, so you can wander the community garden and see the range of farm operations that use the land as part of the trust's Farms for the Future initiative. A number of excellent nearby farm stands beckon, including **KK'S THE FARM** [an organic veggie favorite], **DEEP ROOTS** [help yourself at this charming self-serve spot] and **TREIBER FARMS** [where sustainable ag and art mingle]. In summertime, grab a bucket and pick your own organic berries at **BHAVANA BLUEBERRIES**. To round out a farm-forward day, treat yourself to dinner at **NORTH FORK TABLE & INN**, where fresh inspiration from local farms [and vineyards and waterways] informs chef John Fraser's ever-evolving menu.

MORE THAN 25 ENTRIES ▷

Excerpts have been edited for clarity and concision.

ALMANAC

A deep dive into the cultural heritage of eastern
Long Island through news clippings, timelines,
and other historical hearsay

FARMING HISTORY

*For centuries preceding European contact, Native American
peoples including the Shinnecock and Montaukett grew crops such as corn,
tomatoes, potatoes and beans on eastern Long Island.*

1640s .... The Shinnecock teach newly arrived English settlers corn planting

1658 .... Country's first cattle ranch is established in Montauk

1840 ...... Island's biggest crop is corn, ahead of oats and potatoes, per census

1844 ...... Long Island Rail Road reaches Greenport; crops can get to New York City in just hours

1850 .... Thanks to the LIRR, market prices for potatoes leap to $0.42 a bushel, from $0.18 just a few years earlier

1870 ...... Long Island Rail Road reaches Southampton

1873 .... The first Pekin ducks are brought to the U.S.; East End duck industry begins to take off in 1880s

1880s ..... Demand for cauliflower in New York City spurs production in Riverhead and Southold

1890s ..... New Yorkers begin building summer homes on South Shore, increasing local market for crops

1931 .... Duck farmer Martin Maurer builds The Big Duck [today a roadside attraction in Flanders]

1937 ...... First annual Long Island Potato Festival is held in Riverhead

1940s .... Up to 80 percent of Long Island farming is dedicated to potatoes

1955 .... Mattituck Lions Club hosts its first Strawberry Festival

1959 ...... Suffolk County duck farming reaches high: nearly 8 million ducks

1969 .... Long Island is sixth-largest potato producer in U.S.

1973 .... Louisa and Alex Hargrave plant Long Island's first commercial vineyard in Cutchogue

1974 ...... Suffolk County begins Farmland Development Rights program to keep land in agriculture

1980s ..... Rising real estate prices make potato farms less viable, pushing out many farmers

1983 .... Peconic Land Trust founded to preserve farms and other lands

1990 ...... Quail Hill Farm, one of the first community-supported agriculture farms, established

1991 ...... Long Island Growers Market founded to run farmers markets

2020 ...... Direct-to-consumer efforts like CSAs and farmers markets help small East End farms weather the COVID-19 pandemic

ARTISTS & WRITERS SOFTBALL GAME

Artists. Writers. The ineffable image versus the definitive word. It's a global rivalry as old as creation, but takes a most whimsical form in East Hampton. Since time immemorial [or 1966, for sure], the two expressive breeds have battled on the softball diamond come summertime. The contest owes its mythic origins to post-World War II pickup games featuring Jackson Pollock and tossed grapefruit. The two sides and annual schedule formalized in the mid-'60s, ushering in a golden era when the likes of Willem de Kooning, Eugene McCarthy, Abbie Hoffman and Florence Fabricant took their turns at plate and bag. The game retains this miscellaneous celebrity aura: Governor Clinton of Arkansas, umpiring in '88; Lauren Bacall running the raffle; George Stephanopoulous a reported no-show in more recent years. Jay McInerney and George Plimpton featured on the same powerful 1990 Writers team. Initially a modest fundraiser for doomed liberal presidential campaigns—McCarthy excelled on the diamond, at least—the game now benefits East Hampton causes, doing good locally. As one might expect, arguments about ringers and rules frequently ensue. If we could time-travel to just one summer's afternoon, it would be 1972, when Silvia Tennenbaum, playing with the Artists alongside Dustin Hoffman and Eli Wallach, broke the game's gender line, Plimpton delivered a key hit and the Writers won, though disputes raged.

THE BIG DUCK

Heading down Flanders Road, it's impossible to miss: 30 feet long, 20 feet tall. A wooden frame, cement over wire mesh. A white body, a yellow-orange beak and a pair of Model-T taillights for eyes. Built in 1931, The Big Duck was born of a moment of inspiration: hoping to advertise their Pekin ducks in, well, a big way, duck farmer Martin Maurer and his wife took a cue from a coffee-pot-shaped coffee shop they saw on a visit to California. At the time, duck farming was a growing business on the East End: by 1969, more than half the country's ducks came from Suffolk County. [That number has since dropped to less than 15 percent.] Today, The Big Duck is a gift shop and museum. And its influence spreads far beyond its wingspan: In 1968, architects Robert Venturi and Denise Scott Brown coined the term "duck" to describe architectural forms whose designs, like the duck and the coffee pot, reflect their function. The Big Duck's medium is the message, a larger-than-life reminder of a time when duck farms thrived on Long Island.

BONACKERS

"Speakin' Bonac: Echoes of Dorset?"
The East Hampton Star, April 21, 1977

The speech of Bonackers—the people "B'low the Bridge" and north of the railroad in East Hampton Town—has given rise to reactions ranging from derision to imitation, the reaction seeming to depend upon whether the listener chooses to see the persistence of the dialect as a result of "poverty, no education, too many babies, and too much alcohol," as it has been put, or as local color.

What the speech of Bonac is, from the linguistic viewpoint, is a dialect that retains a surprising number of features of the Dorset dialect spoken by some of the early families who settled in Three Mile Harbor and Springs— Bennetts and Kings, for example—with a substantial number of features of the Kent dialect, and possibly other English dialects thrown in for good measure. The Bonac rendition of "Get up and put a fire under the kettle" ["Giddup an' pud a fuh-yur unda th' kidl"] is, with only one fairly insignificant difference, exactly what a speaker of the old Dorsetshire dialect would have said as late as 1946. The one difference is that the Dorset speaker would have used a light [retroflex] r sound in the word "under" rather than the r-less form common along the entire Atlantic Coast of the United States.

In Dorset the words "wilfully,'" "gradually," "ordinary," "interesting," and "suicide" were pronounced "wilf'ly," "gradjully," "ordnerry," "in trustin'," and "su-cide."

Bonackers, however, seem to have gone Dorset folks one better. In hurrying to tell a tale, they delete entire unstressed words, as a typical Bonac narration attests: "Can' remember who was got throwin' beer can out car."

The Bonacker who says "git" for "get," "yit" for "yet," "turrble" for "terrible, "awchit" for "orchard," "winnuh-ry" for "wintry," "goolp" for "gulp," "achkteck" for "architect," "op-m" for "open," "eeb-m" for "even," or "widduh" for "widow" is speaking a language his ancestors—and his recent counterparts in Dorset—would have attuned to. The adjective "terrible" is much used in old Dorset speech, incidentally.

What probably should be said in general of the Bonac dialect is that it retains many of the usages and pronunciations that were apparently part of the speech of early settlers here. Some of these forms, common and "correct" enough in earlier days, fell out of favor as other forms developed greater prestige. If Bonac dialect features die out—as well they may—perhaps we shall be somewhat the poorer for it.

LONG ISLAND RAIL ROAD

Report of the Board of Directors of the Long Island Rail Road Company to the Stockholders, January 1, 1845

In December, 1843, the board announced to the Stockholders that vigorous measures were in progress for the completion of the eastern part of the Railroad, extending from Suffolk Station to Greenport, a distance of 52 miles. They have now the pleasure to apprise them that the entire line is opened, and has been in successful operation through its whole extent since the 29th day of July last. Two new hotels, to accommodate three hundred guests, are being finished at Greenport; and such are the advantages it possesses from its superior harbor, and the facilities for shooting, fishing and bathing in its vicinity, and its contiguity by railroad to New York, that it must continue to increase. It should be remarked with regard to Greenport, that an opinion has been very freely and generally expressed, by those most competent to judge, that it possesses advantages, in every respect, equal to Newport, Rhode Island, and may now be considered the most attractive spot in the Northern States—its proximity to the Ocean and Gardiners Bay—its climate, and the ease with which it may be reached, after the close of business in the city, in $3\frac{1}{2}$ hours, will make it all that can be desired as a watering place, or as a casual resort from the city.

> *On the South Fork, the LIRR extended to Bridgehampton and Sag Harbor a few decades later, in 1870. From the 1880s to the 1920s, a shuttle train [nicknamed the "scoot"] connected the two forks.*

GROUNDNUTS

Both Accabonac [a harbor and creek in East Hampton] and Sagaponack [a village in Southampton] take their names from an Algonquian term for "land of the big groundnuts." *Apios americana*, a small tuber, grew plentifully on precolonial Long Island. Other names include:

WILD BEAN	POTATO BEAN	PIG POTATO
INDIAN POTATO	BOG POTATO	HOPNISS

SEAFOOD OF NOTE

LARGEMOUTH BASS

The island's temperate climate and many lakes make it a great habitat for the largemouth bass. To sound more in the know, call them "stripers."

....

WHITE PERCH

This small but mighty fish is found throughout the rivers and creeks that feed the Long Island Sound and the Great South Bay.

....

FLUKE

Long Island is rich with fluke, a wide, flat fish, of many varieties, such as winter flounder, summer fluke, and yellowtail flounder. A year-round favorite.

....

BLUE MUSSELS

All along the Long Island Sound, blue mussels attach to hard surfaces like rocks, docks and boats. Rising water temperatures have sadly done a number on these once-plentiful bivalves.

....

BAY SCALLOPS

Called the "jewels of the bay," these button-sized, fleshy shellfish are harvested from the Peconic and Great South bays from November through March.

....

BLUEFISH

The island may be best known for its bluefish, which navigate the waters all year and are loved by hobby and commercial fishers alike.

....

OYSTERS

There are lots of Long Island varieties, but the most celebrated is the Blue Point, harvested from the Great South Bay since the early 19th century.

Though we enjoy them as a delicacy, oysters are bottom feeders: they act as filters before they're harvested, helping to keep our waterways healthy. So, when changing weather patterns and increasing pollution threatened their populations, the state and notable Long Islanders, including Billy Joel, invested in seeding the area's bays and estuaries with more oysters.

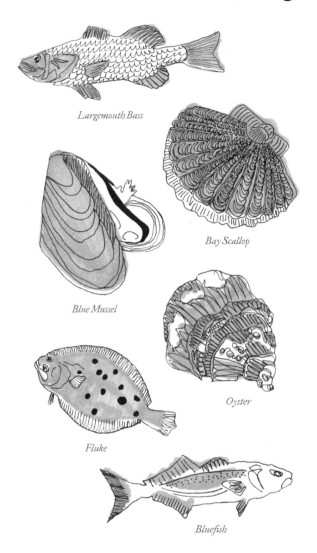

Largemouth Bass

Bay Scallop

Blue Mussel

Oyster

Fluke

Bluefish

JACKSON POLLOCK AND LEE KRASNER

The abstract expressionist artists Jackson Pollock and Lee Krasner moved to Springs, then a remote part of East Hampton, in 1945, shortly after getting married. There, Pollock created his famous drip paintings. The couple lived and worked in Springs until Pollock died in a car crash a decade later; Krasner stayed on until her death in 1984. Below, excerpts from a 1972 interview with Krasner.

ON WHETHER OR NOT IT WAS A DISADVANTAGE TO BE A FEMALE ARTIST

"That's a rough question. Let me put it this way: it hasn't been easy going. But I'm still not clear as I'm speaking to you now whether it has been because I'm a woman artist or because I am Mrs. Jackson Pollock so that I feel in that sense it's more than what's known as a double load. That is to say, if I were Lee Krasner but had never married Jackson Pollock would I have had the same experience I have being Mrs. Jackson Pollock?"

ON NOT BEING OFFERED A RETROSPECTIVE IN THE U.S.

"That's true. I haven't been offered a retrospective here in this country. But I was offered one in England which I accepted and was very happy to be able to see a large span of work. This is terribly important for the painter, I think, because it's the only occasion on which you can see a real period of work before you. Now why I wasn't offered one I would say is a combination of the fact—or maybe I'd have to say principally because I am Mrs. Jackson Pollock. You've got to remember that Pollock is dead now since 1956 and that I am the executor of his estate. Consequently I behaved with the paintings as I saw fit. I stepped on a lot of toes. And I think even today it's difficult for people to see me, or to speak to me, or observe my work, and not connect it with Pollock. They cannot free themselves. So this may be one of the reasons I've not been offered a show. I wouldn't know if there are others."

—*Oral history interview with Lee Krasner, 1972. Archives of American Art, Smithsonian Institution.*

RECOMMENDED READING
Lee Krasner: A Biography by Gail Levin, 2011
Jackson Pollock: Energy Made Visible by B.H. Friedman, 1972

WALT WHITMAN

*In 1862, Walt Whitman devoted the final installments of his
Brooklyniana column in the* Brooklyn Standard *to his East End travels.
Below, an excerpt from his October 11 column on a sailing
trip out of Greenport.*

The black-fish were biting famously, and I stood at the end of the dock, quite proud of a big fellow I had just hauled up; and baited my hook again with "fiddlers," while the fish floundered at a great rate around my feet. Just then a party of lively girls, conveyed by a clerical looking personage, and one or two younger fellows, came down the wharf, and betook themselves on board a taut and tidy sloop fastened there. Some large baskets also made their appearance. It was evidently a party off for a pleasure sail. "Ease away your lines for a moment," said the young sailor who was working the sloop, to me and my companions, "till we shove along the pier." I obeyed, and asked him where he was bound. "To Montauk Point," he answered—adding, with sailor-like frankness, "Won't you go along?" Upon the word, accoutred as I was, I plunged—the fish—into an old tin kettle, and gave them, with sixpence and my direction, to a young sea-dog, and jumped aboard. As we pushed our sloop off from the pier's sheltering bulwarks, the wind struck her, bellying out her sails and tilting her down on one side in a decided and beautiful style, quite to the water. I expected a few little screams, at least, from the young ladies, but these East Long Island girls are terraqueous, like the men; long before our jaunt was over, I discovered that they could give me head-start and beat me all hollow in matters connected with sailing. It was a very pleasant and sensible party; the girls were unaffected and knew a hawk from a hernshaw, and the minister laughed and told stories and ate luncheons, just like a common man, which is quite remarkable for a country clergyman. I found him one of the pleasantest acquaintances I had yet made on the island. We sailed along at a stiff rate—told anecdotes and riddles, and chatted and joked, and made merry. As for me, I blessed my lucky stars; for merely to sail—to bend over and look at the ripples as the prow divided the water—to lie on my back and gaze by the half-hour at the passing clouds overhead—merely to *breathe and live* in that sweet air and clear sunlight—to hear the musical chatter of the girls, as they pursued their own glee—was happiness enough for one day.

LONG ISLAND POTATO QUEEN

The Patchogue Advance, August 18, 1960

Long Island has a brand-new, 1960-model Potato Queen in the attractive person of 18-year-old Carole Lee Squires. She was chosen from a group of six finalists Saturday night at the third annual Potato Blossom Ball in Riverhead. The pert and pretty daughter of a fourth-generation Water Mill farm family received her crown from a one-time schoolmate, Miss Joanne Borkoski, also of Water Mill, the Long Island Potato Queen for 1959. Miss Squires, a vivacious brownette whose beauty of face and figure is enhanced by a sparkling personality, is the daughter of Mr. and Mrs. Carlos L. Squires and the oldest of five children. A June graduate of Southampton High School, she will enter the School of Nursing at Southampton Hospital in September. She was selected by a panel of judges, who had their work cut out for them in assessing the six attractive candidates, on the basis of pulchritude, poise and personality. The 1960 Potato Queen, who was adjudged by her Southampton High School classmates to be the girl "with the nicest smile," is a skilled tractor operator and frequently pitches in and helps with other work on the Head-of-Pond Road, Water Mill, farm which has been continuously operated by her family for over 150 years.

BOBBY VAN

Bobby Van, born Robert Craig Van Velsor, was famed as both restaurateur and pianist at Bobby Van's in Bridgehampton, from its opening in 1969 until he sold the place in 1986. The devoted clientele included writers like Truman Capote, George Plimpton and Kurt Vonnegut. [Capote could often be seen waiting for the restaurant to open at noon, anxiously anticipating his first of many "orange thingees": four parts vodka, one part orange juice.] Artists Roy Lichtenstein, Warren Brandt and Willem de Kooning drank there as well, and Dustin Hoffman was the rare drop-in allowed to play the piano. Van preferred all jazz and swing, all the time at his establishment, though Bob Dylan himself once took up the piano to play an early rendition of "Catfish." Bobby Van died in Nassau County in 2007, at the age of 64.

CONSCIENCE POINT

*In 1640, a small group of English colonists arrived on Long Island,
at a site known ever since as Conscience Point. Below, an excerpt from
the deed that formalized the settlers' purchase of 8 square miles—
the start of today's Southampton—from the Shinnecock Indians,
who had lived there for hundreds of years.*

This Indenture made the 13th day of December Anno Dom. 1640, between Pomatuck, Mandush, Mocomanto, Pathemanto, Wybennett, Wainmenowog, Heden, Watemexoted, Checkepuchat, the native Inhabitants and true owners of the eastern part of the Long Island on the one part, and Mr. John Gosmer, Edward Howell, Daniell How, Edward Needham, Thomas Halsey, John Cooper, Thomas Sayre, Edward ffarrington, Job Sayre, George Welbe, Allen Bread, William Harker, Henry Walton, on the other part, witnesseth, that the sayd Indians for due Consideration of sixteen coats already received, and also three score bushells of Indian corn to be paid vpon lawfull demand the last of September which shall be in the yeare 1641, and further in consideration that the above named English shall defend vs the sayd Indians from the unjust violence of whatever Indians shall illegally assaile vs, doe absolutely and forever give and grant and by these presents doe acknowledge ourselves to have given & granted to the partyes above mencioned without any fraud, guile, mentall Reservation or equivocation to them their heirs and successors forever all the lands, woods, waters, water courses, easemts, profits & emoluments, thence arising whatsoever, from the place commonly known by the name of the place where the Indians hayle over their canoes out of the North bay to the south side of the Island, from thence to possess all the lands lying eastward betweene the foresaid boundes by water, to wit all the land pertaining to the partyes aforsaid, as also all the old ground formerly planted lying eastward from the first creek at ye westermore end of Shinecock plaine. To have & to hold forever without any claime or challenge of the least title, interest, or propriety whatsoever of vs the sayd Indians or our heyres or successors or any others by our leave, appointment, license, counsel or authority whatsoever, all the land bounded as is abovesaid. ... Before the subscribing of this present writing it is agreed that ye Indians above named shall have liberty to breake up ground for their vse to the westward of the creek aforementioned on the west side of Shinnecock plain.

CLASSIC HAMPTONS HOMES

TRAVERTINE HOUSE *East Hampton*

Gordon Bunshaft designed the iconic 1963 modernist house on Georgica Pond for himself and his wife—his only residential design. Simple and low-slung but light filled, all glass and bright white. Torn down in 2004.

....

HALCYON LODGE *Southampton*

Part of the original Southampton Village cottage colony. One of few extant 19th-century stick-style Victorians. Once belonged to Henry Ford, who commissioned a glass addition in 1946.

....

DOUBLE DIAMOND HOUSE *Westhampton Beach*

Andrew Geller's 1959-commissioned creation embraces sharp cubist lines characteristic of midcentury modernism—literally in the shape of two upright diamonds.

....

COXWOULD *East Hampton*

Harrie T. Lindeberg's trademark thatch-like roof shingle design was meant to evoke the old English cottages of the Cotswolds.

....

GWATHMEY HOUSE *Amagansett*

Three-level design build of cubes, occasional curves and a double-height living room with sharply angled roof. Designed by Charles Gwathmey, one of the New York Five.

....

SALTZMAN HOUSE *East Hampton*

Rounded corners, all white, designed to fill with sunlight. Architect Richard Meier built upon Le Corbusier's principles regarding space and form.

....

PINWHEEL HOUSE *Water Mill*

The walls of Peter Blake's 1953 creation were installed on tracks so they could open and close, creating a sense of permeability [and the option of closing up completely when stormy weather demanded it]. From above, with the walls slid open, it resembled a pinwheel.

....

BECKER HOUSE *Wainscott*

Irish farmhouses inspired the slanting stone facade, which gives a fortress-like appearance to this 1969 house in a former potato field. Architect Norman Jaffe designed more than 50 Hamptons houses.

LONG ISLAND VITICULTURE

In 1973, Louisa and Alex Hargrave began planting their eponymous vineyard, which became the first commercial vineyard on Long Island. Since then, dozens have followed in the Hargraves' footsteps, the majority on the North Fork. Though chardonnay and merlot form the backbone of the industry, cabernet franc and sauvignon blanc earn more attention, and wineries continue to search for grape varieties that can thrive here—in a region that contends with frost, high humidity and the threat of tropical storms during harvest, as well as the impacts of climate change. As recently as a decade ago, most local wineries broadcast their similarities to Bordeaux, both in terms of grapes planted and growing conditions, and marketed their wines by comparing them to those of other regions, like Burgundian chardonnay. The winemaking reflected that promise, with many trying—through the use of new oak barrels and long extraction times—to make wines that tasted as good as those from more established regions. At best, the results were poor facsimiles of wines made elsewhere. Today, winemakers have gained the confidence to scale way back on that more manipulative style, instead favoring the distinctive flavors and textures born of well-grown Long Island wine. The best East End wines have a food-friendly freshness that make them ideal partners on the dinner table, particularly with local produce, duck and seafood from the surrounding waters.

MONTAUK PROJECT

A fake Apollo Moon landing. Child abduction for psychological research. Encounters with extraterrestrials, Nazi scientists, reptilian beings and Jesus Christ. All these appear in a series of books that Preston Nichols wrote with Peter Moon. According to Nichols, these accounts came from his own recovered memories of the "Montauk Project," a series of shadowy government experiments that he and other conspiracy theorists believe were conducted at Camp Hero, or Montauk Air Force Station, between 1971 and 1983, to develop techniques for psychological warfare, time travel and teleportation. Though widely debunked, these stories inspired the hit Netflix show *Stranger Things*—*Montauk* was an early working title—and informed parts of Thomas Pynchon's postmodern detective novel *Bleeding Edge*. The site is now Camp Hero State Park, though the staunchest believers claim that experiments continue in a subterranean facility.

RUM RUNNING

"Sea Strategy! An Untold Story
of How Four Coast Guard Cutters
Captured the Fleetest of
Rum Runners"

Brooklyn Daily Eagle,
February 5, 1930

The Francis, king of the liquor-running speedboats, was captured not long ago by Uncle Sam off the eastern tip of Long Island. On the morning of the epic capture, about a month ago, the Francis was sighted near Ruins Gas Buoy off Gardiners Island, coming at slow speed with muffled engines.

Glance at a map of eastern Long Island, the busiest smuggling area in the world. Imagine four Coast Guard boats waiting patiently in line between Gardiners Island and Plum Island.

The invisible quartet allowed the Francis to pass through the center of the line. Then the CG 401 went through the ritual of stopping a vessel at sea, first throwing her searchlight on the Coast Guard flag to identify the challenging party, then throwing the light on the boat challenged, firing blanks as warning to stop and finally solid shot across the fleeing rum-runner's bow.

For a second there was no shooting in earnest. One of the rummies was still scrambling about on the deck of the Francis. The rule of Coast Guard Base Four, at New London, where the four Government boats came from, is no shooting while men are visible. When the man disappeared from sight the sputtering of machine guns began from the two nearest Coast Guard craft.

In that first burst of firing the captain of the Francis, a man named Green, was seriously wounded by a bullet which penetrated the hull.

As the Francis tore toward freedom, it let loose an eye-biting acrid smoke screen made by the simple process of pumping castor oil at high pressure in a spray through the exhaust pipes of the engines.

The four pursuing boats coughed their way through the smoke. Their strategy, predetermined, was to run straight ahead, like four fingers stretching straight to the west.

The speedier Francis, dodging diagonally, soon found itself cut off by the northernmost Coast Guard boat. The king wheeled in his wake and shot south, hoping to escape around Gardiners Island.

This time the Francis was cut off by the southernmost Coast Guard boat. There was nothing to do but run for it, around the northern side of Shelter Island, which is set like an apple between the teeth of the V-shaped mouth with which Long Island snaps at the Atlantic.

There was no shooting now, nor had there been after the flurry at the beginning, for the Coast Guard gunners were afraid of hitting each other in the dodging.

It is also a curious fact, worth a short digression, that the duels between law-breakers and law-enforcers on the high seas are more of wits than of lead.

A chief petty officer once gave us the Coast Guard feeling.

"We may hit some one when we fire but we are not anxious to do so. Guys on classy boats like the Francis are sober, decent fellows, taking a chance for big money. Anyway, killings make us unpopular with the public."

A mobster at Greenport told us that he expects to be shot at. He said:

"We expect a shellacking. So long as they don't hijack us, that is, shoot without going through the ritual, we got no kick coming. Lying between the Liberties or behind armorplate is safe enough. Of course, if a bullet gets a gasoline feed line, fire starts and then it is just too bad.

"Why didn't we stop when warned? Don't make me laugh. The Big Boss can get plenty of men for $15 a night who will stop when warned. We get $400 for delivery."

Such are the opposing codes of rum-running today.

With the Francis far in front, the CG 401 next and two others following, the chase passed Greenport. The game of tag continued into Southold Bay.

A desperate run to the south almost let the Francis clear, but the CG 822, anticipating such a move, had gone around Shelter Island the other way and was waiting as a reception committee of one.

[It is worth noting that Coast Guard boats bearing numbers in the 800's are usually converted rum-runners which have been seized by the Government.]

It was ironical that a former liquor boat should prove the nemesis of the Francis, which had outraced and outfoxed so many regulation Government boats in the past.

Trying to skirt Cedar Beach Point in a strong cold wind blowing right on the beach, and thus evade the CG 822, the Francis went aground.

The crew of the smuggler escaped, carrying with them their wounded captain. The vessel proved to contain 492 sacks of whisky which were seized and trucked to the Army Base in Brooklyn.

The Francis was patched, taken to New London for repairs and eventually was escorted to the barge office in Manhattan, and there forced to jostle with lesser liquor lights until the owners were able to take advantage of legal technicalities and get possession again of the king.

SAG HARBOR WRITERS OF NOTE

JOHN STEINBECK
Steinbeck wrote *The Winter of Our Discontent* in the octagonal writing studio of his waterfront cottage on Bluff Point, which he owned from 1955 until his death in 1968. He was fond of bringing his miniature poodle, Charley, to the bars, and dressing as a fisherman in hopes of going unnoticed.

....

SPALDING GRAY
The Rhode Island-born monologist wrote most of his work, including his best-known monologue *Swimming to Cambodia*, in the Victorian home on Madison Street where he lived with his family. His 1995 book *Morning, Noon and Night* details his life there.

....

THOMAS HARRIS
Harris created Hannibal Lecter and wrote *Silence of the Lambs* above Marty's Barbershop on Main Street. Harris still spends his summers in Sag, where he can frequently be found at The American Hotel.

....

BETTY FRIEDAN
In the late 1970s, the legendary feminist writer and activist bought a cottage on the shore of Upper Sag Harbor Cove, where she lived for nearly 30 years until her death in 2006. She could be seen jogging down Glover Street or playing at the beach with her grandson.

....

COLSON WHITEHEAD
Two-time Pulitzer winner Colson Whitehead and his wife, literary agent Julie Barer, live part-time on Swamp Road, between Sag Harbor and Northwest Harbor. Whitehead drew inspiration for his 2009 novel *Sag Harbor* from his own teenage summers there.

> *Sag Harbor's historic Black community, which dates back to the 1930s, centers on three subdivisions: Azurest, Nineveh, and Sag Harbor Hills. "According to the world, we were the definition of paradox: black boys with beach houses," Colson Whitehead writes in* Sag Harbor. *"A paradox to the outside, but it never occurred to us that there was anything strange about it. It was simply who we were."*

NAZI SABOTEURS IN AMAGANSETT

The East Hampton Star, July 2, 1942

The eyes of the whole country have been turned on Amagansett, since Saturday night, when the dramatic announcement came over the radio that eight Nazi agents had been landed from submarines—four of them at Amagansett, four near Jacksonville, Fla., on June 13; and that all eight had been captured. The FBI made the announcement, but the FBI and Coast Guard co-operated in apprehending the Nazis. These men, whose pictures have appeared in the New York papers, were trained graduates of a Nazi school for saboteurs; they are said to have buried four large cases of bombs, TNT, detonators and other equipment in the sand at Amagansett [near the bathing casino at the Beach Hampton development], after coming ashore in the heavy fog in a rubber boat. The submarine is said to have brought the men to within 500 yards offshore. The men carried large sums of American money, wore civilian clothes, and had with them plans for a two-year program of destruction of industrial plants, railroads, waterworks and bridges stretching from New York to the Middle West. Although eastern Long Island had been full of FBI men for two weeks following the saboteurs' landing, relatively few people here had any idea that anything unusual was afoot. Now that the story is at least partially public property, many are recalling events of that foggy Friday night and Saturday, when visibility was so poor that you could hear boats close offshore but could see nothing. The story, even when it was told in a public place that very night after it had happened, sounded so fantastic that hardly anyone believed it. The story goes that a young Coast Guardsman came upon the four invaders; challenged them but was unarmed; that they discussed killing him then offered him a bribe of over $200 to keep his mouth shut; that he sped to the nearest phone and notified headquarters; but by that time the Nazis had disappeared. He then led the Navy and FBI men to the spot where the evidence was dug up, and his information led to the capture of the criminals. That is the unconfirmed story. There is material for any number of Hollywood thrillers, or hair-raising detective yarns, in this thing that has happened under our very noses. It is fantastic, but it can and did "happen here." Something happened, at least. Full particulars will probably go unrevealed until after the war.

The captured agents were tried by a military commission in August 1942. Six of the eight were executed. No other German saboteurs attempted landings in the U.S.

GREY GARDENS

The cult classic 1976 documentary *Grey Gardens* paints an intimate portrait of the two reclusive Edith Beales—a memorable mother-daughter pair better known as "Big Edie" and "Little Edie"—as they live in squalor in a run-down East Hampton mansion. An aunt and cousin, respectively, of Jacqueline Kennedy Onassis, Big Edie and Little Edie had occupied the once-grand Grey Gardens for decades as they free-fell from high society following Big Edie's divorce. The film has a haunting, gothic quality, revealing the mansion to be falling apart, home to countless feral cats and rambling raccoons. But the women themselves remain witty and stylish, even while Big Edie disinterestedly narrates a cat defecating behind her portrait or Little Edie tells of the many romances that failed due to her mother's disapproval.

> *Big Edie passed away in 1977; Little Edie in 2002.*
> *In 1979, Little Edie sold Grey Gardens to journalist Sally Quinn and* Washington Post *editor Ben Bradlee, who restored it. Fashion designer Liz Lange now owns the property.*

THE SAGG MAIN SET

When Peter Matthiessen, the only author to win the National Book Award in both fiction and nonfiction, bought his house in 1959, Sagaponack was a quiet community dotted with farms and small homes. Over the next two decades, solitude, beauty and cheap rents—this was before mansions lined the shore—drew legions of writers and artists to the area, including luminaries like Truman Capote, *Paris Review* co-founder [with Matthiessen] George Plimpton, Kurt Vonnegut, E.L. Doctorow, Robert Caro and James Salter [who ventured a little farther east to Amangansett]. *Vanity Fair* dubbed the crew the "Sagg Main Set" for the road linking Sag Harbor to Sagaponack. The group played touch football in Matthiessen's yard, dined and, of course, boozed together, often at saloon Bobby Van's. Matthiessen and Salter, who swam together on summer evenings at Gibson Beach, remained close friends for decades. "When you celebrate Christmases together and everyone's birthdays and other events through the years," Salter wrote for *The New Yorker* in a remembrance of Matthiessen after his death in 2014, "a dense and indestructible fabric is made, really too rich to imitate or describe."

THE LONG ISLAND EXPRESS HURRICANE

On September 21, 1938, the Great New England Hurricane ripped through eastern Long Island. The storm earned the nickname "The Long Island Express Hurricane" because island residents had no warning and were unable to evacuate. It was one of the most destructive storms ever to pass through the area.

"Brief Hurricane Notes"
The East Hampton Star, September 29, 1938

Mud and water came up to the windowsills, in Forrest Hulse's house and Le Roy King's, on Egypt Lane. Turtles and fish came along with it. Egypt Green has a pond in it. The beautiful willows on Huntting and Egypt Lanes are down; and Mrs. Ruger Donoho's garden is sadly torn, great trees lying on it.

On Friday, the Philip James house on the beach at Amagansett was still cut off by water in the roadways, so that the full extent of damage could not be judged. The windmill was lying on the ground; the porch was off. Smaller cottages beside the road on that part of the beach were sitting deep in water, or overturned.

Miss Gertrude Rackett's summer cottage had its roof torn off at the height of the storm, then the front was ripped off, leaving it standing just like a child's dollhouse, with the rooms and their contents exposed to the street. Miss Rackett was alone in the house, and somehow made her way to shelter at Mr. and Mrs. I.Y. Halsey's. She has now gone to Mr. and Mrs. James Grimshaw's for the winter.

The Brown summer home is in a very exposed spot, on the high cliff just west of Montauk lighthouse; yet, by some freak of the storm, little damage is said to have been done there.

Nearly fifty people from nearby cottages on the dunes here took refuge in the Phelan Beale house, that Wednesday night. Mrs. John Cole, as reported in last week's paper, was ill in bed at her home with bronchial pneumonia; her nurse, Miss Bush, swam for aid from the Coast Guard, braving the terrors of oncoming waves and terrible wind. She told the Coast Guardsmen that Mrs. Cole must be kept dry, or she would not answer for the consequences. They carried her out, put her into a boat without exposing her to a bit of water; and her fever dropped with the storm, she is now very much improved.

MONTAUK LIGHT

By Charles Parsons
Harper's Magazine, September 1871

We reached Montauk Light, and the end of our second day's tramp, a little after dark. Later in the evening we accompanied the keeper [Mr. Ripley] on a tour of inspection. Going through a passage-way we found ourselves in the oil-room, neatly paved with colored tiles, the oil being stored in large tanks on one side of the room. The ascent is by one hundred and thirty-seven steps, winding around the central shaft, and the walls are of enormous thickness; the tower, erected in 1796, was some years since strengthened by building a solid brick lining inside of the original structure. Immediately below the lamp is the keeper's room and the apparatus which keeps the revolving "flash" in operation. Here through the long weary watches of the night, one hundred and eighty feet above the sea, exposed to the full force of the wild Atlantic storms, these faithful sentinels keep vigil. On their fidelity and constant watchfulness depends the safety of the many thousand vessels that annually traverse this highway of the sea.

A few steps higher and we are in the lantern, containing a "Fresnel" flash light of the first order, made by Henry Lepante. It is a miracle of ingenuity in the scientific concentration of the lenses. We step inside the lenses as the "flash" slowly revolves, and the next moment are inclosed in light which is visible thirty-six miles seaward. The flash throws a flood of brilliant light around the entire circle, disappearing and re-appearing every two minutes.

Stepping out on the balcony that surrounds the tower, the glorious panorama of the moonlit sea lay all about us, and at that moment two ships were crossing the glinting light of the moon. The raw, chilly night air soon drove us below to the comfortable fireside of the keeper's family, where we sat listening to stories of storms from the southeast, during which the whole weight of the Atlantic is thrown directly upon Montauk Head. The light-house is built of granite, and, founded on a rock, stands on the bluff sixty feet above the beach. The sea is silently eating its way toward the tower, and this will soon compel a removal to the higher ground west.

WHALERS OF NOTE

Whale hunting was integral to Indigenous cultures on Long Island and became a major industry after colonization, with Sag Harbor and Greenport serving ocean-going whalers. Islanders also practiced "shore-whaling" close to land.

AUSTIN HERRICK	Lore-laden captain: tales of Brazil shipwreck, jungle exploits, Southampton happily-ever-after.
MERCATOR COOPER	Southampton's Cooper Hall namesake, famed for sailing every sea, early visit to feudal Japan.
POLLY GARDINER	Reportedly the first Long Island "whaling wife," aboard the *Dawn*, 1820s.
DAVID WAUKUS BUNN	One of many Shinnecock people involved in the trade. Drowned on the *Circassian*, 1876.
PYRRHUS CONCER	Black whaler, formerly enslaved, joined '49er California gold rush. Returned to Southampton homestead.
GEORGE WHITE	After a long 19th-century career, including Arctic explorations, settled to become a farmer/activist, protecting South Shore beaches.

Jeanette Edwards Rattray, longtime publisher of The East Hampton Star, *described historic whaling practices in the journal* New York History *in 1933: "In Southampton anyone reporting a whale ashore was rewarded with 10 shillings. … If a whale should be sighted on the Lord's Day, the reward was not payable. It was not seemly, in those days, even to walk upon the beach on the Sabbath; and if whales were strewn its entire length no one would touch them on that day."*

PLUM ISLAND

About a mile and a half off of Orient Point, at the far eastern end of the North Fork, lies a mostly pristine, and mostly secret, island. Secret because the island belongs to the U.S. government, and the developed portion of it contains the Plum Island Animal Disease Center, a highly restricted site established in 1954 by the Department of Agriculture. The center is dedicated to combating infectious diseases in livestock. And, as the center's director Larry Barrett told *The New York Times* in 2016, "Food security is national security." A plan is in motion to relocate the animal disease center to Manhattan, Kansas. For several years, that plan included opening the island to development—the Trump Organization expressed interest in building a golf course—but local groups fought to block the sale. The island, also home to a decommissioned Army fort, provides habitat for endangered species and contains lands important to the history of Indigenous peoples. In 2020, the Trump Administration signed legislation that will prevent the public sale of Plum Island, putting it on the path to permanent preservation.

EINSTEIN THE SAILOR

In the summer of 1939, heavy thoughts occupied Albert Einstein's mind. From his summer home on the North Fork, he sent a letter informing President Franklin D. Roosevelt that "it may be possible to set up a nuclear chain reaction in a large mass of uranium" and urging Roosevelt to "speed up the experimental work" of U.S. physicists. No surprise, then, that the man took to the water for solace and sailing. But he was not, by all accounts, a great sailor. "Here's a tippy little bit," the Mattituck *Watchman's* Patter column reported, on July 20. "Professor Einstein, while sailing about the Old Cove, was overtaken by a bit of a puff and very rudely turned over. Our intellectual neighbor sat calmly on the overturned boat and awaited the rescue party." And a couple weeks later, on August 3, in a column called The North Forker: "A genius relaxes. Princeton's Professor Einstein out sailing Saturday and taking no chances. His small sail was reefed to the size of a postage stamp. But he was as happy as the captain that overtook him in a much faster boat."

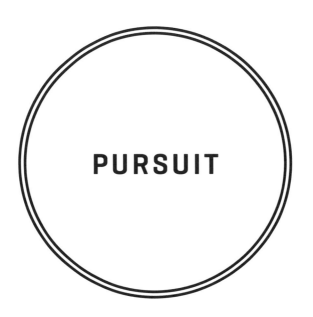

PURSUIT

A field guide to farms on the East End, with geological background, a close look at the seasons, insight from farmers and a curated selection of farm stands and markets

FOUNDATIONS

Terroir isn't just for wine. On the East End, the sea-influenced climate conditions and the legacy of the last ice age combine to create ideal conditions for agriculture.

GEOLOGY

About ten thousand years ago, the receding Wisconsin glacier left behind the rocks and soils that today make up Long Island. Two ridges of rocky debris [known as terminal moraines] extend across the island's length. Since the ice melted in a northerly direction, the beaches of the North Shore are rocky with deposits left behind by the glacier, while the South Shore's are smooth and sandy. Long Island is part of a region known as the Outer Lands, which includes Cape Cod, Nantucket, and Martha's Vineyard—all of which formed from terminal moraines around the same time.

SOIL

The retreating glaciers left behind deposits rich in minerals—mica, granite, quartz—making for excellent soils. Bridgehampton silt loam, the dominant soil type on the South Fork, is smooth and wonderfully fertile. It retains moisture well, which is important for thirsty crops, like the potatoes that were once planted all over the area. Haven loam, which makes up the North Fork's primary topsoil, has a little more sand mixed in with the silt and clay but drains extremely well—good for farms, and great for vineyards.

CLIMATE

Eastern Long Island has a maritime climate, meaning the surrounding waterways keep the temperature within a narrower range than other nearby areas at this latitude. [Thanks to higher average winter temperatures, zone 7 on the USDA's Plant Hardiness Zone Map—which shows what kinds of plants are likely to thrive in different areas—swoops through Long Island before veering south.] The growing season starts later. This is actually a good thing, because it means farmers and vintners rarely have to worry about spring frosts. It also lasts longer, giving crops ample time to grow into their ripest selves. Plus, there's plenty of sunshine.

SEASONAL BOUNTY

What grows on eastern Long Island and what to do with it.

ASPARAGUS *May* The asparagus harvest arrives in early to mid-May. Snap the tips off, blanch the young stalks in salted, boiling water for a few minutes, shock them in ice water and serve with flaky salt.

STRAWBERRIES *June* Strawberries ripen on the North and South forks in mid-June, the first official fruit of the season. Macerate them in a little sugar and top with fresh whipped cream.

SWEET CORN *July* Out east, sweet corn is king. The best way to eat it, no competition: steam it, serve with butter and salt. No one does East End corn better than Amagansett's **BALSAM FARMS**.

TOMATOES *August* Both forks specialize in hybrid and heirloom varieties. Enjoy them sliced fresh, with a sprinkling of salt and torn basil.

POTATOES *September* The East End was once potato country. Few potato farms remain, but **FOSTER FARM** in Sagaponack still grows superlative tubers. [Marilee Foster's spuds also make their way into chips and spirits at the Sagaponack Farm Distillery.]

APPLES *October* On Long Island, apple season runs from fall through early winter. For more than half a century, the Halsey family has tended apple and peach orchards at the **MILK PAIL** in Water Mill. The store sells killer apple cider donuts, so you don't have to make them. Instead, try your hand at a crisp.

HARVEST CALENDAR

	J	F	M	A	M	J	J	A	S	O	N	D
Apples								█	█	█	█	█
Apricots					█	█	█					
Asparagus				█								
Beans					█	█	█	█	█	█		
Cherries						█	█					
Corn							█	█	█	█		
Cucumbers					█	█	█	█	█			
Fresh Flowers					█	█	█	█	█	█		
Garlic	█	█						█	█	█	█	█
Grapes								█	█	█		
Greens	█	█	█	█	█	█	█	█	█	█	█	
Herbs			█	█	█	█	█	█	█	█	█	█
Lavender			█	█	█	█	█	█	█	█	█	█
Peaches							█	█	█	█		
Pears								█	█			
Plums								█	█	█		
Potatoes	█	█						█	█	█	█	█
Raspberries							█	█	█	█		
Rhubarb				█	█	█	█					
Spinach	█	█	█	█	█	█			█	█	█	█
Sprouts	█	█										
Strawberries					█	█	█					
Summer Squash					█	█	█	█	█			
Tomatoes						█	█	█	█	█	█	
Winter Squash									█	█	█	█

HARVEST CELEBRATIONS

Mattituck Strawberry Festival
Mattituck, June

Long Island Garlic Festival
Riverhead, September

Hallockville Country Fair and Craft Show
Riverhead, September

FARMING BY THE SEASONS

SPRING

Whether the farm sows its crops by direct seeding—planting right into the ground—or starts its seeds in a heated greenhouse or barn, early spring marks the start of the growing season for alliums, parsley and hearty greens, including kale, collards and Swiss chard. Nightshades such as tomatoes and peppers come next and, after the last frost in mid-April, root vegetables, herbs, peas and greens. Spring also brings the first harvest of overwintered kale, collards and pea shoots. *Avg. low temps: 30s to 50s; highs: 40s to 70s.*

SUMMER

Leading up to the summer solstice, when days are longest, farms are lush with growing crops and grass. At this point, more than half of a farm's crops are planted so they can enjoy and store plenty of sunlight for post-solstice, when night begins to creep in earlier. In July, garlic planted the prior fall is harvested and seeds are started for brussels sprouts, cabbage, broccoli, cauliflower and chicories. Farm stands and markets brim with summer squash and zucchini, melons, tomatoes, peppers, sweet corn and cucumbers. *Avg. low temps: 60s; highs: 80s.*

FALL

The East End's climate is the mildest in the state, so autumn is the most beautiful time. Apples are picked—by families seeking a weekend activity, and by farmers who will move their harvests to cold storage to last the year—and garlic is planted. Farmers begin to harvest their July plantings or move them into greenhouses. The last of the root vegetables endure a frost or two—converting starches into sugars to withstand winter—and are harvested by early December to end the year on a sweet note. *Avg. low temps: 50s; highs: 70s.*

WINTER

The quiet forces farmers, usually so dedicated to working the land, to slow down. These colder months provide the time to catch up on tasks that may have gone undone through the more fruitful seasons: to focus on neglected machinery and tools in need of repair and tend to cover crops—like barley, rye and pea shoots—that are grown throughout the year. Inside the greenhouse, farmers replant cold-hardy crops like spinach, arugula and other lettuces. *Avg. low temps: 10s to 30s; highs: 40s.*

FARM STANDS

The freshest places to find farmers selling what they grow.

MARILEE'S FARMSTAND
Sagaponack
Remarkable heirloom tomatoes from the Foster family's six-generation potato farm.
....

MILK PAIL
Water Mill
Home to Amy's Flowers, dreamy cider donuts. "Here Today" list tells what's fresh.
....

KK'S THE FARM
Southold
Area's only spot for biodynamic fruit and veg. Fresh-cut sunflowers too.
....

AMBER WAVES FARM
Amagansett
Market, cafe and farmlands open to wandering. Close enough to smell the sea.
....

SANG LEE FARMS
Peconic
Lee family's farm began as a 1940s Chinatown supplier; now grows organic greens and herbs.
....

WOWAK FARMS
Laurel
No-frills stand known for sweet corn, asparagus and iconic hand-painted sign.

LATHAM FARMS
Orient
Briny air and fresh produce at the tip of the North Fork for over 200 years.
....

PIKE FARMS
Sagaponack
Tomatoes, sweet corn and more on farmland saved with the Peconic Land Trust's help.
....

TREIBER FARMS
Peconic
Sustainability and creativity fuel this self-serve spot run by father and son, Peter Sr. and Jr.
....

DEEP ROOTS FARM
Southold
The honor system rules at a farm featuring pasture-raised pigs and chickens.
....

BALSAM FARMS
Amagansett
Tomatoes galore, excellent corn, jarred goods and a top-notch CSA.
....

GREEN THUMB
Water Mill
Organic produce and plants on land cultivated by the Halsey family since the 1660s.

WE ONLY
SELL
WHAT WE
GROW

SPECIALTY

U-PICK VEGGIES
Cooper's Farm Stand

Mattituck

Pull a wagon into the field, where green beans, asparagus and bell peppers await.

....

CHEESE
Mecox Bay Dairy

Bridgehampton

Handmade raw-milk cheeses. Try the creamy Atlantic Mist or nutty Mecox Sigit.

....

EGGS
Browder's Birds

Mattituck

Organic eggs at the farm stand and via CSA. Visit to meet chickens, ducks and sheep.

....

U-PICK FRUIT
Wickham's Fruit Farm

Cutchogue

Berries, apples, peaches and pumpkins on land cultivated since the 17th century.

BERRIES
Oysterponds Farm

Orient

Known for naturally grown blueberries, raspberries and blackberries, all perfectly ripe.

....

POULTRY
Feisty Acres

Southold

Began with pasture-raised quail; now also chukar partridge, French guinea fowl and more.

....

U-PICK BLUEBERRIES
Bhavana Blueberries

Southold

Blueberry bushes cover more than 30 acres. Fill your bucket in July and August.

....

FLOWERS
North Fork Flower Farm

Orient

Two tucked-away acres of fresh herbs, grasses and flowers, including 10 dahlia varieties.

FARM & BUTCHER SHOP
8 Hands

Cutchogue

Organic produce, grass-fed meats, yarn spun from the farm's Icelandic sheep flock.

....

HERITAGE
Hallockville Museum Farm

Riverhead

The farm where the Hallock family lived for 250 years now preserves North Fork agricultural history.

....

PRESERVATION
Invincible Summer Farms

Southold

Grows rare and endangered heirloom tomatoes and peppers; maintains a vast seed bank.

....

CHARITY
Share the Harvest

East Hampton

Nonprofit farm donates what it grows to local organizations feeding those in need.

COMMUNITY SUPPORTED AGRICULTURE

QUAIL HILL FARM *Amagansett*

One of the country's first CSA programs when it was established in 1990, Quail Hill has a hands-on approach: members come dig their own tubers and cut their own greens, consulting a colorful chalkboard to see what's ripe. As Scott Chaskey, head farmer for three decades, wrote in *This Common Ground*, "As members of the farm walk and harvest in the fields they begin to recognize land as a community to which they belong." In 2020, director Layton Guenther worked with the Bridgehampton Child Care and Recreational Center's Bonnie Michelle Cannon to distribute excess produce through a Farm to Food Pantry program.

....

SYLVESTER MANOR EDUCATIONAL FARM *Shelter Island*

A farm where land preservation meets the future of food. Bread shares and egg shares available too.

....

BIOPHILIA ORGANIC FARM *Jamesport*

A sample late-summer share's variety: tomatoes, cabbage, potatoes, Swiss chard, ground cherries, tomatillos and okra.

....

SEP'S FARM *East Marion*

Produce shares large and small, with flexible veggie substitutions to make sure you like what you get.

FARMERS MARKETS

Most are open from May to November. Check before you go.

EAST HAMPTON FARMERS MARKET
Fridays, 9 a.m.-1 p.m.

MONTAUK FARMERS MARKET
Fridays, 9 a.m.-2 p.m.

SAG HARBOR FARMERS MARKET
Saturdays, 9 a.m.-1 p.m.

WESTHAMPTON BEACH FARMERS MARKET
Saturdays, 9 a.m.-1 p.m.

HAVENS FARMERS' MARKET (SHELTER ISLAND)
Saturdays, 9 a.m.-12:30 p.m.

SOUTHAMPTON FARMERS AND ARTISANS MARKET
Sundays, 9 a.m.-3 p.m.

FARM-TO-TABLE RESTAURANTS

Local growers provide plenty of inspiration for East End chefs.

ALMOND
At the two-decade-old Bridgehampton institution, chef and co-owner Jason Weiner makes hot sauces to use up some of the abundant, end-of-season peppers that grow at Amagansett's QUAIL HILL FARM.

NORTH FORK TABLE & INN
Michelin-starred chef John Fraser's curated wine list showcases local vineyards. Wines from RGNY, HOUND'S TREE and MCCALL are all available by the glass.

NICK & TONI'S
Executive chef Joe Realmuto shops from his own garden, adjacent to the famed restaurant's parking lot. The names of nearby farms like Amber Waves and BALSAM, with which Realmuto keeps close relationships, pepper the menu as it changes with the seasons.

PAWPAW
Taylor and Katelyn Knapp—who also head up the popular Peconic Escargot brand—are responsible for the Greenport pop-up known as PAWPAW. Dates are announced sporadically, and the food, served in courses, showcases the riches of the North Fork's bays, farms and vineyards.

18 BAY
Housed in a charming 1893 post office and general store, Elizabeth Ronzetti and Adam Kopels' Shelter Island restaurant is so driven by what's available at farms like Sang Lee, Wickham's and ZOMBIE FREE that they change their multicourse menu every week.

CONSIDER THE PIZZA

At AMBER WAVES FARM's summer pizza nights in Amagansett, you can make your own pie almost entirely from the farm's own abundance: the garlic, basil, tomatoes and the wheat—hence the name—that makes the crust.

PERSPECTIVES

"Our family has been farming here for 12 generations. The Milk Pail building on Montauk Highway was built in 1972, and we've been growing and selling our apples and pumpkins and various other little projects along the way. On the farm, nothing's ever the same. Yes, you have the same four seasons, and you're planting the same types of pumpkins or taking care of the same trees. But something always comes up. The weather changes. Regulations change. Equipment breaks. So there's always a challenge around the corner. But it's an awesome way to live."

—**JENNIFER HALSEY DUPREE**, Milk Pail

"At Treiber Farms, we're trying to open up the space to people to come and do their best work here. We started an artist residency. We've also had a series of dances, music in the old barn, independent film screenings, workshops in natural dyeing and cooking classes. I've worked with chefs, traditional visual artists, brewers and distillers—just trying to constantly collaborate with folks who do really cool things. This blend of agriculture and the arts is what I've been striving for from the beginning. "

—**PETER TREIBER JR.**, Treiber Farms

"My mother bought Loaves and Fishes in 1980, and I'm now the owner. Writing the farm series—12 books, one for every month, celebrating ingredients from the farms we buy ingredients from—some of them were a huge eye-opening experience for me. I'd challenged myself to get to know the local farmers in a better way, and understand why they're growing what they're growing. I marvel that people are still farming. From one generation to another—it's amazing."

—**SYBILLE VAN KEMPEN**, Loaves & Fishes and Bridgehampton Inn

"The farm was started by two brothers, Henry and Gurden Pierson Ludlow, in the 1870s. In the 1950s, the family had to get rid of the cows and go full-scale into potatoes. Around 2000, Dad started the dairy again, this time selling cheese locally instead of milk, which made all the difference. The decisions we make are very long-term. It's sustainability: preserving the legacy as much as preserving the actual environment of the farm."

—**PETER LUDLOW**, Mecox Bay Dairy

INCLUDED

INTERVIEWS

---

*Ten conversations with locals of note about starting a farm,
land preservation, Jackson Pollock's legacy, surfing,
Shinnecock identity, winemaking and more*

AMANDA MERROW

FARM CO·FOUNDER

FARMING BY THE sea just feels like how it ought to be. There's a magic about it.

THIS LAND USED to be owned by Pat Struck, who ran the Amagansett Farmers Market here for many decades. She sold it to the woman who preserved it, Maggie de Cuevas, who then sold it to us.

SO YOU COULD say the farm has been women-owned for 75 years.

AMBER WAVES IS a special place because we have 10 agricultural acres that are located on a sidewalk in a village, which is a pretty unusual thing.

IT'S REALLY IMPORTANT to us to have this be open access. Usually it's really bustling with families who are here to visit the chickens and walk around and just enjoy themselves.

MY PARTNER, KATIE, and I met doing a farm apprenticeship at Quail Hill Farm in 2008. It was before the interest in artisanal grains had really hit.

SO WE WERE like, "Maybe we could have a bread farm, or a pizza farm."

WE STARTED WITH that idea, but also immediately grew vegetables.

I REALIZE, in hindsight, how unlikely it was that Katie and I would succeed at this.

IT DIDN'T OCCUR to us that it was a pie in the sky idea.

WHY WOULDN'T WE be able to start a farm here, in one of the most expensive places in the country, and make it work?

THESE DAYS WE grow about 300 varieties of 60 crops of vegetables, flowers and herbs.

WHEN WE STARTED farming, I remember feeling totally swept off my feet by the work.

I WAS SO gripped by it that I couldn't imagine not doing it, couldn't imagine doing anything else.

HELEN A. HARRISON

ART HISTORIAN, CURATOR

WHEN JACKSON POLLOCK and Lee Krasner moved to Springs in 1945, the population was 300. It was all farmers, fisherfolk and tradespeople.

THEY ACTED AS the magnet. A lot of their artist friends came out. There are over 50 artists living in Springs now.

THE BARN IS where Jackson did all of the poured paintings that are now so famous. He would lay the canvas out on the floor.

WHEN WE MADE it into a museum, we removed the covering and exposed all of the colors and gestures that he left that spilled over the edges of his pictures.

AFTER HE DIED in '56, Lee moved in, and it became her studio for the rest of her life.

BOTH OF THEM worked without sketches. It had to be spontaneous.

WHAT'S THE EXPRESSION? You're playing the violin while you're building it.

I STARTED AT the Parrish Art Museum in Southampton, then later became the curator of the museum here in town, Guild Hall. In 1990, I was hired to direct the Pollock-Krasner House.

MY HUSBAND JOKES that my next stop is the Montauk Lighthouse, and then it's burial at sea.

WHEN I WAS at Guild Hall and working as an art critic for *The New York Times,* I would meet Lee at openings, or I would call her up for a quote. It was always very cordial, but she was not an easy person.

PEOPLE WANTED THINGS from her. She was his sole heir; she had to manage the estate and her own career. She wasn't going to just become the Widow Pollock, the gatekeeper.

WHEN PEOPLE GO to a museum, they see the paintings, the sculptures. When they come here, they connect to the human presence behind the art.

JOHN V.H. HALSEY

LAND TRUST PRESIDENT

MY ROOTS RUN deep here.

HALSEYS GO BACK to the origins of Southampton, one of the English families that came in 1640. I'm 12th generation.

WE'RE SORT OF like rabbits. In my graduating class in high school, there were more Halseys than Smiths.

THERE WAS A tremendous increase in property values out here in the '70s and into the '80s, really fueled by second-home development.

IN 1980, I was living in San Francisco, and I came back to spend four to six weeks here.

I SAW A for-sale sign on our neighbor's farm—a family farm that had been passed on for 10 generations. Their parents had passed away, and they had a $2.2 million federal inheritance tax.

I WAS 28 years old. I wasn't thinking very much about estate taxes.

THEY ESSENTIALLY sold the farm to pay the tax, and with the penalties, they ended up with next to nothing.

THAT WAS A seminal event for me to want to return here and to create an organization that would work with landowners before they got into that position.

I MADE IT back in '83 and, with four other people, founded the Peconic Land Trust.

OUR MISSION IS working farms, natural lands and heritage.

FOOD PRODUCTION and access to food are really important.

WHAT WE'VE SEEN here over the last 40 years is a real diversification of agriculture: out of wholesale production, into a lot of retail sales and farm stands and farmers markets.

IN SOME RESPECTS, farms have probably become more relevant to communities today than they were 50, 60 years ago.

TONY CARAMANICO

SURFER, ARTIST

WHEN I STARTED surfing, I sort of knew what I wanted to do the rest of my life.

I'VE BEEN LIVING in Montauk since 1971.

MONTAUK WAS VERY quiet, a sleepy little fishing village that closed down after Labor Day.

IT'S DEFINITELY the premier surfing spot in New York. It's one of the most consistent surf breaks on the East Coast because we stick out there and we have all these rocky points and coves.

WE HAD A pretty strong surf community. Now we're all the old buggers. But back then, we kind of ran the show.

I DID SOME competition. I had surf shops—my first surf shop in 1971 was called the Albatross, which evolved into a restaurant and a motel.

THEN I WORKED for Peter Beard for seven years, starting in 1978. He was the man about town in Montauk during that era.

EVERYBODY WAS AT his house, from the Warhols to the Kennedys. I got to meet lots of interesting people.

AT THE TENDER age of 41, I turned pro. I traveled the world.

MY ARTWORK IS my surf journals from living that lifestyle.

PETER TOLD ME to keep a journal. But being around Peter, you just don't keep a daily diary. It became an artistic endeavor.

AFTER 20 OR so years of keeping these journals, I was approached to be in a gallery. It took off from there.

I'M 71 NOW. I am still surfing, but my body's telling me it's getting harder all the time.

I'M LOSING MY edge, if you will. It's kind of tough to not be a really good surfer anymore.

BONNIE MICHELLE CANNON

COMMUNITY LEADER

GROWING UP HERE, we know all the secret places.

. . . .

WE KNOW HOW to get around. We know all the back roads that you all don't, so in the summertime we can get from Southampton to Bridgehampton in 15 minutes, when it's taking you an hour.

. . . .

BRIDGEHAMPTON WAS different then. It was a village and it was a community of people of all ethnicities that pretty much got along, though there was separation: there was a Black neighborhood, and there was a white neighborhood.

. . . .

YOU COULDN'T JUST do anything as a child around here and get away with it because everybody knew everybody.

. . . .

THE BRIDGEHAMPTON Child Care and Recreational Center is a historically Black community-based organization serving minorities, those that are marginalized, those in need.

. . . .

THE CENTER IS a diamond in the rough; it's a safe haven.

WE'RE REBRANDING, SO we'll be called "The Center" versus "Bridgehampton Child Care and Recreational Center." We are so much more than that.

. . . .

WE HELP PEOPLE with their journeys and with their issues. And we personalize it.

. . . .

RIGHT NOW, the big challenge is affordable housing.

. . . .

I AM THE chairperson for the town of Southampton's housing authority, and I'm also a commissioner for Suffolk County Human Rights Commission.

. . . .

MY FAMILY HAS always been about service and helping people. That's all I've ever seen, both with my family and with the individuals who lived in the neighborhood.

. . . .

EVERYBODY HELPED EACH other. Everybody gave. Everybody served.

. . . .

TO SHOW LOVE, to be love, that's all I know. That's my foundation.

MARILEE FOSTER

FARMER

FOSTER FARM WAS once a very large potato farm. My brother Dean and I are sixth-generation farmers here.

IN THE EARLY '90s, we were seeing how quickly the potato-scape was changing.

THERE'S ALWAYS GOOD and bad years in farming. You expect that, especially when you're in a single crop.

I STARTED RAISING exotic vegetables in the late '90s and started a small farm stand.

I LOVE MY time outside. I'm obsessed with tomatoes. As they say, farming's a great lifestyle, if you can afford it.

WE REALLY BECAME a farm in transition in the last five years.

POTATOES ARE DIRTY, they're heavy, you don't necessarily love it all the time, especially when you're young—so the distillery idea was always a joke: *Boy, it'd be great to turn these things into vodka.*

DEAN AND I started this project in 2013. We realized, in order to stay doing what we wanted to do, we had to come up with another strategy, another business plan.

WHICH WAS THE distillery.

OUR GOAL IS to make beautiful spirits and to share, in a very— no pun intended—distilled form, the real sweetness of this place, which is its land.

EVERYTHING WE END up bottling I could give you an essay on, because it's all hooked into my family: what we've done, what we grow here.

PEOPLE OFTEN SAY to me, *Oh, wouldn't this be worth more as houses?* Everybody assumes you're always going for the highest and best dollar.

FARMERS ARE JUST going for the right dollar to keep going.

IT'S SOMETHING THAT came before you, and it's going to be here after you.

PERRY GUILLOT

LANDSCAPE ARCHITECT

WHEN YOU LIVE in Southampton, you feel as though you haven't left New York. It's really a greener version of the city.

I TRY TO plant a landscape, not build it.

THERE'S AN APPRECIATION for a softer palette of materials. Not so structured; no gratuitous wall features.

WHEN I FIRST came out here many years ago, I remarked how one plant knitted together the public view of so many of these towns into one unified roadside experience.

ONE PLANT PULLED together the whole landscape, or at least what you see from the road in the residential sections of town.

PRIVET IS ALMOST like the silly putty of the plant world. You can push and pull it and personalize it.

IT'S PLANTED TO provide visual screening. It never made sense when there were 5-acre lots—it was more of a windbreak.

NOW IT'S A barrier between neighbors, because the houses are taller and they're closer. It's tremendously more important.

MY BOOK, *Privet Lives,* was a bit of a comedy in that I used the privet to infer who the people in the house would be by how they treated their hedge.

IT BECAME THIS fairy tale, but the whole story was about global warming, if you can believe it. And I did that in 1998.

I TOLD THE history of Southampton going back 18,000 years. But underneath is a metaphor of man's treatment of the natural environment.

THE HEDGE BECOMES the thing that separates him, physically and emotionally, from the natural environment.

THAT IS WHAT'S happening in the bigger story of the planet.

SHANE WEEKS

CULTURAL CONSULTANT, ARTIST

MY TRADITIONAL NAME is Bizhiki Nibauit. That means Standing Buffalo.

I GREW UP on the Shinnecock Reservation. I did a lot of hunting and fishing, walking through the woods, hanging out with friends, riding bikes.

THERE WAS A sense of freedom.

MY INTEREST IN history, in culture—it was something that was always there. In elementary school, I spent my time in the library, checking out encyclopedias.

PARTICULARLY FOR OUR own culture: I wanted to know who I was as a Shinnecock person.

MY DAD TAUGHT me how to dance, and about our history. He was the dean of admissions at Nassau Community College for quite some time. So I get that interest in education from him.

OUR TEACHINGS AND history are not isolated to Long Island.

Traveling to other communities throughout the Northeast, into Canada, out to the Great Lakes, down South—they all have bits and pieces of our story.

I AM CO-CHAIRMAN of the Shinnecock Nation Graves Protection Warriors Society, and our primary focus is preserving sacred sites, particularly burial grounds.

WE RECENTLY WERE able to preserve one of our most sacred burial grounds, Sugar Loaf Hill.

OVER THE LAST couple of years, I've been creating films that bring awareness to who we are as Shinnecock people.

UP UNTIL VERY recently, people always heard about who we were from the media. It wasn't our words, and it wasn't always accurate.

IN THE AGE where information can be instantaneously transmitted, first-person, that has really helped to spread awareness of who we are.

APRIL GORNIK

ARTIST

I AM PROUD to be an East End resident.

MY HUSBAND, ERIC Fischl, and I built a house for ourselves in 1999. We still thought that we were going to be going back and forth to the city.

IN THE WINTER of 2004, we ended up staying. We realized that we really loved it out here and didn't want to go back.

WE'VE BEEN SURPRISED, gradually, finding out how many amazing painters and other artists there are out here, including in Sag Harbor.

IN 2017, WE knew that there was a big old Methodist church at the other end of town from the water, on Madison Street.

IT HAD BEEN deconsecrated and on the market for about 12 years when we got to it.

ERIC HAD A tremendous fantasy about trying to have an artist residency in Sag Harbor. And I desperately wanted to save the church as something that the community could participate in.

SO IT ALL came together in this amazing, serendipitous way.

WE RENOVATED The Church and opened the doors in spring of 2021. In our programming, we're celebrating local art and art history and the history of Sag Harbor.

ERIC DID BEAUTIFUL portraits that replaced the stained glass windows. People who showed creativity in their lives, in their work process, and made a huge difference in the lives of others because of their dedication to their work.

THEY'RE OUR NEW saints.

I NEVER GET into my studio first thing in the morning. I just try to make sure that I'm in there every day.

THERE'S SO MUCH that gets embedded in a painting.

Especially the way I paint, because it's not a splash of color, splash of color. Mark, mark.

IT'S A MASSIVE amount of underpainting, and then adding on top of the underpainting. Then working that out, and then deciding when whole areas of a painting have got to go. Then redoing it or changing it.

IT JUST GOES on and on and on.

THE LAST PAINTING I did took, I swear, over three months. I just kept redoing it and redoing it. I couldn't feel my way through it.

SOME PAINTINGS, you'll start, and they'll just paint themselves.

IT'S LIKE, *That was pleasant. Thank you. Couldn't they all be like this?* Invariably, the next one is just like, *Either this painting goes, or I do.*

THERE'S NO GUARANTEE of what's going to happen when you're working. It's just an essential part of making art.

THERE'S A BIG soul component to being in my studio for me, just to try to keep myself together.

IT IS A spiritual, psychological refuge for me—even though it's really frustrating and really challenging and never gets easier.

THIS IS THE thing that's blown my mind the most, having worked this long in essentially the same genre of painting.

IT'S STILL JUST as hard to start a painting, and just as frustrating, and leads to unexpected delights and many, many, many unexpected challenges that are just enough to make you lose your mind.

BUT IT'S just part of the process.

IF WE CAN transmit some of that sense of frustration and satisfaction of the creative process to people who are coming to The Church, to give them a sense of hope and ability and invention and real positive persistence, that'll be a real gift to people.

KAREEM MASSOUD

WINEMAKER

PAUMANOK VINEYARDS was founded by my parents, Charles and Ursula Massoud.

MY MOTHER WAS born and raised in the Pfalz in Germany, which is a big winemaking district. She has relatives who are still vintners there.

MY FATHER WAS born and raised in Lebanon. His family was involved in hospitality, so he was surrounded by a culture that enjoyed fine wine.

RIGHT AFTER I was born, we moved to Kuwait—the last place you would think of wine. It's literally and figuratively a dry country.

MY FATHER started making his own, as he put it, out of necessity.

MY PARENTS fantasized about becoming vintners in Germany, but instead my father got transferred to New York.

HE READ ABOUT Alex and Louisa Hargrave, the pioneers on Long Island as far as wine.

SO HE LOOKS at my mother, and he says, "We might be able to do this in our own backyard."

THEY PLANTED OUR first vines in 1983. I was 10 years old. I remember walking behind my father, dropping a stake behind every vine that was planted.

FOR MOST OF the '80s, we were just growers, selling the crop to our neighbors.

THEN 1988 HAPPENED, and it was really an excellent vintage. That spurred my parents to finally move forward with building the winery and making our own wine.

THE FIRST BROCHURE for our winery had language like "The beginning of a tradition." I thought, *How can you say it's the beginning of a tradition?*

BUT MY PARENTS knew exactly what their aspiration was: to be a multigenerational fine wine estate.

WE'RE HAPPY AND proud of what we've accomplished so far.

STORIES

Essays and selected writing from
noted East End voices

MEMORY AND SALT SPRAY: A PLACE OF LAYERS

Written by **SCOTT CHASKEY** | *Dawn, almost, though a waning crescent moon rises in the east, just preceding the sun, over the tangled hedge, over the tallest reach of the larch. The sky, an ocean of light, like a tide returning. To the south a thin river of mist caps the newly seeded field of rye. Here in the garden, within the net of moon-ocean-earth, every living thing reflects like a jewel. The auburn tips of timothy grass, the three-pointed leaves of liquidambar, the red clusters of Sichuan peppers, the vines of* Apios americana *intertwined on young conifers. All that is flooded with dew flickers in the early light. There is something in the flight of the sparrow hawk, in her quick fall from the hedgerow to alight on silt loam, something familiar, remembered, just so, as daylight fills the furrows.*

One night this past autumn I camped out in a back field, to witness the beginning of another day, and I awoke to discover those words. I know the field well—I seeded a cover crop of rye here in 1990, my first year of farming at Quail Hill in Amagansett. In my book entitled *This Common Ground*, a narrative that threads through the seasons on the farm, I began with this sentence: *In a peninsular place the clarity of light is partly what lures the lover of land and water*. It is that same clarity that has drawn artists of all sorts to the fishtail of Long Island. I witness it—the light—daily, and luckily I am not yet *accustomed* to it. Once I saw an ecstatic performance—choreographed by the autumn setting of the sun and the precise amount of ocean moisture required to set a hedgerow of sassafras, olive, honeysuckle and bittersweet ablaze. The image, like that of the crescent moon rising before the sun, is etched in my memory.

This land is surrounded by water and it was carved by water. When the Wisconsin ice sheet retreated 11,000 years ago, great blocks of ice pressed and melted into the earth to form kettle holes, and the glacial motion left deposits of mineral rock, sand and loam that formed a backbone of low hills known as a terminal moraine. Long Island Sound, too, was once a hollow carved by ice that later filled with water, a waterway that served as a conduit for ancient peoples and cultures.

I am new to this island, *fish-shape 'Paumanok*, the name preferred by the good gray poet, Walt Whitman, who was born here near *the rolling sands and drift, the leaves of salt-lettuce left by the tide*. I say "new" though I have worked the soil of Amagansett daily for over 30 years, with an eye open for the red-tailed hawk, the osprey, the killdeer nesting on our soil surface, the red-winged blackbirds returning in March to nest in cedars and to announce spring. John v.H. Halsey, who founded the Peconic Land Trust, a conservation organization that has preserved over 13,000 acres on the East End—my employer for three decades—traces his lineage in Southampton back to 1640. My friend and former apprentice, Bennett Konesni, who founded another innovative local not-for-profit, Sylvester Manor Educational Farm, is an 11th-generation descendant of Nathaniel Sylvester, resident at the Manor on Shelter Island in the 1660s. I am fortunate to have worked with members of the Shinnecock Nation ["People of the Stony Shore"], coastal Algonquians, indigenous to this place 10,000 years before the arrival of Europeans. This island was home to at least 13 Native tribes at one time, and the flukes of the fishtail now known as the South Fork and North Fork were the territory of the Shinnecock, the Montaukett and the Manhasset. Today the Shinnecock Reservation consists of 800 acres bordering a tidal inlet, now under threat by the rising tide of climate disruption.

This is a place of layers, just under the surface glitter of the Hamptons: generations of silt loam and tidal meadows, and generations of families, tribes, hamlets and towns awash with historical memory and salt spray. This is a place of diverse habitats: pine, oak and beech forests, inland ponds, maritime grasslands, tidal wetlands, salt marsh, miles of sandy beaches, and the walking dunes at Napeague. Those unfamiliar with this island are amazed—as I continue to be—that a narrow strip of land jutting out into the Atlantic can also contain superb growing soils. I respect the wisdom that the real health of a bioregion resides in the first 6 inches of topsoil; if only we counted our wealth here by that measure alone. Sift a handful of Bridgehampton silt loam through your fingers, smell it, or better, plant into it, and with some guidance from a grower, you will be witness to one of our Earth's finest gifts: fertility.

When I first arrived here I was told by several salt-of-the-earth farmers—and I acknowledge their warning and despair—that farming is dead on Long Island. Three decades later, I beg to differ. True, thousands of acres of prime soils, which for years yielded up mountains of potatoes, have been swallowed up—lost to development, covered over by ostentatious second homes that remain vacant for much of the year. The tide continues to change, though: Thousands of acres are now preserved, protected, cultivated by more than a few tenacious families and a growing stream of smart, dedicated, passionate young people, and the land yields tomatoes, squash, greens, garlic, herbs, 50 other crops, and still some spuds that supply local farmers' markets, restaurants, schools and food pantries with fresh food. When our land trust surprised the farming community, over three decades ago, by introducing to the East End something called Community Supported Agriculture, we were assisted by the only organic farm then in business, the Green Thumb of Water Mill. Now, over 50 organic or regenerative farms are making good use of our good soils, and teaching others to do so.

My account of this land/seascape is slanted toward the soil—like my mentor, Edgar Wallis, who worked the cliff meadows on another headland, the Cornish Penwith Peninsula, for a long lifetime, I can say: *I took to the land!* For a more balanced view, I invite you to follow the work of my friend and fellow island citizen Carl Safina, who took to the sea. In *The View from Lazy Point*, he writes: *In the cycle of seasons and waves of migrating fishes and birds that come and go along my home coast, I still find sanity, solace, and delight.* I once stood next to Carl on a landing that abuts an expansive tidal pond and estuary. Among others, we were there to wonder at a pod of dolphins that had entered the salt pond [on the map, a tidal creek] only to become stranded. The scene before us was strange, eerie, and no one knew what had called the dolphins here. We were a community united in our compassion for another species: agile, intelligent mammals with so much to teach us. We can search for sanity through mystery as well, and this land/seascape in its diversity offers that at every turn of the tide.

I would like to bow to the solar and earthly cycles that inspire all forms of water to move, and to the impulse of our planet to carve the land we presently occupy: North America/Turtle Island, Long

Island/Paumanok. I began this piece at dawn, and I will close with the swallows' hour.

Dusk: a bright moon rises in the east over the north Atlantic. The ocean is near, I hear it, just there beyond the railroad tracks and Amagansett village—a short glide for an osprey. I am surrounded on every side by robust maples, white pines, an elegant larch, a thick tangle of bittersweet, honeysuckle, and the rampant porcelain berry, as I kneel on the sweet-smelling earth, planting beans as the light fades: New Mexico, Tuscarora Bread, Rafioffi, Purple Stardust, Shinnecock. As the first star appears below the moon, fireflies rise among the grasses, flickering like earthly stars, on familiar terms with this soil. Swallows dip off toward night, and I press the last of the varietals one by one neatly into the row. This silt loam remembers the moment, as do I, as the last of the seed, Nightfall, fills the furrow. Flash! a firefly, as the living seed, too, remembers the silt.

SCOTT CHASKEY is a farmer, poet and educator. A pioneer of the community farming movement, Chaskey served as director of Quail Hill Farm in Amagansett for three decades. He is the author of the books *Stars Are Suns*, *This Common Ground* and *Seedtime*. His next book, *Soil and Spirit*, will be released by Milkweed Editions in 2023.

THE WORTH OF WAMPUM

Written by **ANDRINA WEKONTASH SMITH**

I AM OUT TO DINNER with my mother and stepfather at Fellingham's, a Southampton community mainstay with good food and a fuss-free atmosphere. Decades worth of Little League photos line the walls of an interior that has stayed the same since my childhood.

Walking anywhere in Southampton with my 60-year-old mother is a test of one's patience. As an unofficial mayor of the village, she can't walk very far without bumping into some she knows—and after we eat, she spots her kindergarten teacher at one of the outdoor tables. While we chat, a glint of purple catches my mom's eye: discarded quahog shells sitting on the table. Already acquainted with the Shinnecock's affinity for wampum, my mother's teacher is happy to share them with us, and she makes sure we take "the ones that are nice and purple." Walking to the car, my mother hands me some of the shells, and I laugh. Leaving Fellingham's, while holding the discarded clam shells of my mother's kindergarten teacher, is the Southampton I have always known.

Shinnecock means "People of the Stony Shore." When the tide is right, large stones emerge from our shores, offering captivating views that make that name well-earned. Growing up in a coastal, tribal community, we've always viewed the beach as an extended family member. Shinnecock banter about our "clam-digging toes" can often be heard on our tribal beaches in the summer as family members compete to see who can get the most clams. I remember summer days spent in clam competitions with my friends and cousins. I would walk through the water with a corkscrew-like stride, feeling for any clams that might have burrowed into the sand—a strategy that I still use today.

Wampum, or *wampumpeag,* is the name of the intentionally carved

pieces of clamshells that have maintained significance to countless generations of Eastern Woodland people. Historically, wampum was made by coastal tribes like Shinnecock and was used as a part of ceremonial exchange, trade or to convey a message's significance. Early Dutch and British colonists' perception of wampum as currency grew out of their misunderstanding of this exchange.

Incorporated in 1640, Southampton is one of the oldest villages in the state of New York and, therefore, the country. Its winding back roads began as horse-drawn carriage routes and Native American footpaths. The award-winning beach views were once quarries that yielded bountiful amounts of wampum, with the Long Island Sound in particular producing it in vast abundance. That abundance was often given as tribute to larger tribes, like the Narragansett of Rhode Island, whose great numbers were able to offer protection to smaller tribes. Today, the Narragansett are still one of Shinnecock's sister tribes [the Unkechaug Nation on the Poospatuck Reservation in Mastic, New York, is the other].

In the absence of a consistent European currency, colonizers came to view this as a viable form of trade with the Indigenous populations, and wampum even became an official currency of the Massachusetts Bay Colony in 1650. But when the Dutch began to flood the market with cheap beads, and coins from lucrative West Indies trades circulated on the island, wampum's reign as currency for the colonists ended.

Of course, that was never how wampum was used among tribal communities. For both historical and modern Shinnecock people, the significance of the shell cannot be overstated. It's still common for a person to save a shell with prominent purple to adorn their home, use for smudge with sage or sweetgrass, or include in traditional crafts.

Wampum is a marked sign of honor and pride. When my cousin Shesha turned 18, I gifted her with a pair of wampum stud earrings to mark the occasion. When tribal member Autumn Rose Williams won Miss Native American USA in 2017, she did so wearing a wampum crown. In the winter of 2022, when Lubin Hunter passed away at the age of 104, his going home ceremony had his coffin and hands holding wampum to help ensure a safe journey to the spirit world. Wampum made by Shinnecock wampum master Chuck Quinn adorned his neck.

* * *

Hidden on a quiet pathway on the reservation, Uncle Chuck's driveway is nearly indiscernible: only a rusted mailbox marks the entrance. But like so many places on the reservation, there is a vitality. It feels entirely unlike the manicured lines and tall hedges surrounding the McMansions in the village, just a mile away. The reservation includes some of the most beautiful, undeveloped land anywhere in the Hamptons. As Shinnecock, we are the entrusted stewards of this land, and that role has been passed down from generation to generation. However, with our homelands now comprising some of the most expensive real estate in the country, our burial grounds are in danger of being developed, and the glacial pace with which the town has moved on the matter of agreed-on return triggers a PTSD 382 years in the making.

When I get a third of the way down the driveway, I get out of my car to open the long metal gate that keeps trespassers out and Uncle Chuck's large dog, Buffalo, in. When I reach the house, Uncle Chuck is already outside working. I show him the shells that my mother did not keep, and he tells me to throw them in the yard. On the ground, broken shells of various sizes can be seen, embedded into the soil of the driveway. This is just one of the many strategies he uses to break down the large shells into smaller pieces—work smarter, not harder. When a piece is ready to reveal itself, it shall.

Uncle Chuck's yard is an homage to his craft, and I never tire of its many treasures. An elaborate wampum workstation rests in one corner of the yard, and large buckets containing shells at various stages of the process line the yard's edge. In addition to dropping off the extra shells my mother didn't need, I came to pick up a few necklaces for friends making their first visit to Long Island's shore. It's a tradition I first began while completing The Watermill Center's residency program [an international artist laboratory], and one that I've maintained since. Uncle Chuck's wampum is a representation of a raw side of the East End that visitors rarely see. Carrying a piece of it is a way of carrying our story, of carrying a piece of our waters with you.

He brings out assorted trays of wampum. Leather strings of various lengths hang from the hand-drilled holes in the shelves. I see which pieces speak to the personalities of my friends, and one in particular jumps out at me. It's from the section of the shell that has traditionally been discarded. People want smooth shells, rounded beads or flat discs. The misshapen edge of this piece of the shell provides none of these and is often a challenge to include in crafts. In Uncle Chuck's hands, however, I've seen this underestimated piece of wampum take on the shape of dolphins, claws or teeth. When I wear my necklace made of these precise pieces, I know that value is all about perspective. Like my ancestors, and so many Shinnecock people today, I know what wampum is actually worth.

ANDRINA WEKONTASH SMITH is a storyteller from the Shinnecock Nation. She was a 2021 Native American Media Alliance Fellow, a 2021 Netflix Accelerator Grant recipient and a 2021 Guild Hall Community Artist-in-Residence. She has been featured in *Edible East End* and *Native Max* magazine, and she worked with TIME studios as a writer on an immersive VR experience released in 2022. She spends her time between Brooklyn and Southampton, where she is building a tiny house on the reservation.

THE UNSOLD WARHOL

Written by **VALERIE COTSALAS**

This story was originally published in The New York Times *in 2006.
Since then, Warhol's Montauk estate has changed hands multiple times,
but its allure and particularity remain.*

ON THE EASTERN TIP OF LONG ISLAND, 120 miles from Manhattan,
the morning light shines first upon the Montauk Moorlands, a
brooding wind-blown range of craggy bluffs where ocean waves curl
and crash against the rocky shore more than 30 feet below.

It's an extreme place compared with the rest of Long Island's
South Fork, which is better known for its privet-hedge-entombed
mansions [both old and McNew] to the west and the blue-chip
summer homes on Further Lane in East Hampton that sell at eye-
popping prices—$25 million, $30 million, $43 million—even when
the real estate market elsewhere is soft.

But stark Montauk has always been a draw for the congested souls
of artists, writers and musicians who seek the edge. So it's no surprise
that Andy Warhol, a master of extremes, felt a kinship with Montauk's
topography and lack of pretension. But he also shared Montauk with
the hippest and the hottest names of his time: Halston, Liza Minnelli,
Elizabeth Taylor, the Rolling Stones.

And that's just a small part of the Who's Who that once lounged at
Eothen, then a 20-acre estate in a valley amid the moors that Warhol
and his manager and film collaborator at the time, Paul Morrissey,
bought for about $225,000 in 1971. Mr. Morrissey still owns 5.6 acres
of the estate, with a compound of five homes, a stable and a three-car
garage. The whole windswept collection, with 600 feet bordering the
Atlantic Ocean, is for sale for $40 million.

The revolving door of top East End real estate agents who have
struggled with the listing the last five years includes Tina Fredericks,

the broker who sold Mr. Morrissey and Warhol the property 35 years ago.

In 1971, Warhol was bored with being driven around to see houses and spent most of the time snapping Polaroids of other people in the car, Ms. Fredericks recalled recently. But he perked up as he noticed the "sort of funky air" of the village of Montauk and the Memory Motel.

The village is still a place untouched by Citarella or the pool-blue awning of Tiffany & Company, a rugged fisherman's town where shark-fishing competitions are promoted on signs near the entrance to the village.

Eothen lies outside the village, up a winding dirt road that ends on a 30-foot cliff that overlooks the Atlantic. "I just remember him liking it immediately and buying it—boom, like that," together with Mr. Morrissey, Ms. Fredericks said. But Warhol didn't visit often, she said. "He had a lot of problems with the wind, which took his hairpiece off."

* * *

Perhaps because of the effect on his famous silver wigs [one sold in June at auction for $10,800] combined with the artist's fair skin, Mr. Morrissey said, Warhol wasn't much of a beachgoer. Initially, he "wasn't interested in the house, he was interested in the investment end of it, I would say," Mr. Morrissey said. "Although he got to love the house."

The men were in the process of dividing the property—about 15 acres would go to Warhol, and the rest, including a compound of oceanfront houses, to Mr. Morrissey—when Warhol died in 1987 after gall bladder surgery. The Andy Warhol Foundation for the Visual Arts later donated the 15 acres to the Nature Conservancy, which created the Andy Warhol Preserve in 1993.

But even with its storied history as a retreat for the in-crowd of the 1970s and 1980s—add to the guest list Lee Radziwill; her sister, Jacqueline Kennedy Onassis; the artist Julian Schnabel; and the countless models and actresses who rested their lean, weary selves at Eothen—the houses on the compound are too rustic, many brokers say, to bring $40 million.

The five blue-shingled houses were designed to resemble a camp,

Mr. Morrissey said, but with the best workmanship money could buy when they were built in 1931 for the Church family, descendants of a founder of the Church & Dwight Company, makers of Arm & Hammer Baking Soda. There are 15 bedrooms in all, 7 in the main house.

But to hear real estate agents speak of them, the houses of Eothen are hobbit huts compared with what that big money can buy on Further Lane in East Hampton or Gin Lane in Southampton—the Fifth and Park Avenues of Long Island's East End.

Mr. Morrissey's homes [he stays in the caretaker's cottage when renters are there; Warhol preferred the third cottage west of the main house] were designed with plenty of doors and corridors for ocean winds to whistle through, bearing the smell of the salt and sea into the wood-panel rooms.

STARK MONTAUK HAS ALWAYS BEEN A DRAW FOR THE CONGESTED SOULS OF ARTISTS, WRITERS AND MUSICIANS WHO SEEK THE EDGE.

"You feel the breeze?" Mr. Morrissey said, the wind riffling the brim of his cotton bucket hat as he sat at a table on the patio between the cottages. "This you can't capture in a photograph, no matter how many times you photograph it."

Just then, a tall blond man, looking as if he had sauntered off the page of a Ralph Lauren catalog, walked out of the main house and greeted him. Encounters with summer renters were one of the few times Mr. Morrissey smiled during an hourlong visit on a recent afternoon.

He bristled at too many questions about Warhol and peered at his watch when asked for tales of celebrity high jinks. "People didn't come here for big parties," he said. "People basically came here to relax. It's a place you come to for nature, for a breeze, for beautiful scenic things."

On the other hand, Montauk residents still recall the summer when the Rolling Stones rehearsed songs from the "Black and Blue" album, including "Memory Motel," in the main house.

It's hard to imagine the sound of the wiry rockers with their amps and electric guitars belting out "Memory Motel" beneath the animal

trophy heads, mounted elk antlers and the big dead fish above the fireplace mantel in the living room. There's another fireplace at the other end of the room, aged bluestone slabs for floors and a vaulted ceiling lined with exposed beams.

Mr. Morrissey has kept many of the nightstands, beds and desks that came with the house. In line with the spare style of the homes, they were originally from the nonprofit Val-Kill furniture factory in Hyde Park, N.Y., which was started by Eleanor Roosevelt in the 1930s to provide work for local people.

The other cottages have similar old-salt décor: brick herringbone-pattern floors and walls and ceilings lined with rich wood paneling and built-in shelves.

But for $40 million, buyers want "satin sheets and ice makers and Sub-Zero refrigerators and flat-screen TV's, built-in pools," Mr. Brennan said. "If he would sell it for $25 million, I could sell it for him."

Calvin Klein, the magazine publisher Jann Wenner, Ralph Lauren and the hotelier and developer Ian Schrager have all passed on the house, Mr. Brennan said. "And they all like that kind of rustic stuff, but the price tag was just too much."

Tony Cerio, an agent at Brown Harris Stevens who is now listing the property, said 600 feet on the ocean is Eothen's "big value." It is also built upon solid rock, he said, and doesn't experience the kind of gouged-out erosion seen on higher bluffs.

Most real estate agents agree that the real selling point is the estate's singular eastern oceanfront location.

The houses atop the bluffs at Eothen, an ancient Greek word that means "at first light," could never be built today under the Town of East Hampton's zoning laws, including requirements that each house be on a minimum of 10 acres and set back at least 100 feet from the water.

And nothing can be built around them—in addition to the Warhol preserve, the area is next to more than 100 acres of New York and Suffolk County preserves and parkland.

"It is really one of a kind in many respects," said Htun Han, a partner at the Hamptons Realty Group in East Hampton. "You've got all that privacy, and it's absolutely drop-dead beautiful."

Still, "as much as it's absolutely stunning," he said, switching his tack as do many agents who try to gauge Eothen's value, "it's stark, and really a very raw beauty."

Neighbors—Dick Cavett, Paul Simon and Mr. Schnabel among them—are in houses small in the distance and sitting on their own remote bluffs. Mr. Cavett's house, set back on the higher bluffs to the west, was carefully rebuilt after a 1997 fire and is one of seven Montauk Association homes—Shingle-style cottages designed in the late 1800s by Stanford White.

Some, like Mr. Schnabel, who restored another Association home, first discovered the area as guests at Eothen. "I'm surprised that Julian Schnabel didn't buy it," Ms. Fredericks said. "He rented Eothen for a long time."

The buyer who pays anywhere near $40 million for Eothen is likely to see the beauty in the Colonial Revival buildings and in their rugged Montauk surroundings, she said.

"The materials are very real and honest; it wasn't built for show," she said. "If you like the location and you're really looking for privacy, that's certainly it."

* * *

On Friday, June 24, 1983, Andy Warhol and Halston were on a twin-engine plane flying to Montauk, where Halston rented a house on Warhol's Eothen estate.

The "ride was fast and beautiful—the moon was coming up full, and we flew over all the big houses," Warhol recalled to his personal assistant, Pat Hackett, who included the remarks in "The Andy Warhol Diaries."

The next day in Montauk, Warhol lamented that Liza Minnelli "doesn't come out anymore—she and Halston are still not on good terms. Because she didn't wear Halston to the Oscars."

That entry ends: "But Liz Taylor will be coming out to visit Halston in Montauk soon." At the time she was on Broadway in "Private Lives" with Richard Burton.

VALERIE COTSALAS is a freelance writer based in New York. This story first appeared in *The New York Times* on September 8, 2006.

DIRECTORY
& INDEX

DIRECTORY

ART MUSEUMS & SPACES

Alex Ferrone Gallery *Cutchogue*
The Arts Center at Duck Creek *East Hampton*
The Church *Sag Harbor*
Dia Bridgehampton *Bridgehampton*
Guild Hall *East Hampton*
LongHouse Reserve *East Hampton*
Ma's House *Southampton*
Parrish Art Museum *Water Mill*
Pollock-Krasner House *East Hampton*
Southampton Arts Center *Southampton*
VSOP Projects *Greenport*
The Watermill Center *Water Mill*

LODGING

The 1770 House *East Hampton*
A Room at the Beach *Bridgehampton*
American Beech *Greenport*
The American Hotel *Sag Harbor*
The Baker House 1650 *East Hampton*
Baron's Cove *Sag Harbor*
Bridgehampton Inn *Bridgehampton*
Cedar House on Sound B&B *Mattituck*
The Chequit *Shelter Island Heights*
Crow's Nest *Montauk*
Gurney's Montauk Resort *Montauk*
Haven *Montauk*
Hero Beach Club *Montauk*
The Inn at Orient *Orient*
Lin Beach House *Greenport*
The Maidstone *East Hampton*
Marram *Montauk*
The Menhaden *Greenport*
The Montauk Beach House *Montauk*
Ram's Head Inn *Shelter Island Heights*
The Reform Club *Amagansett*
The Roundtree *Amagansett*
Shelter Island House *Shelter Island Heights*
Shou Sugi Ban House *Water Mill*
Silver Sands Motel *Greenport*
Sound View Greenport *Greenport*
The Surf Lodge *Montauk*
Topping Rose House *Bridgehampton*

LIFESTYLE & DESIGN SHOPS

Aloof Icon *Southampton*
Arni Paperie *Southold*
E-E Home *Amagansett*
Homenature *Southampton*
In Home *Sag Harbor*
LIDO *Greenport*
Love Adorned *Amagansett*
Marika's *Shelter Island*
Mecox *Southampton*
MONC XIII *Sag Harbor*
North Found & Co. *Peconic*
One For All *Southold*
Share With *Montauk*
Sylvester & Co. *Sag Harbor*
Tea and Tchotchkes *Greenport*
touchGOODS *Southold*
The Weathered Barn *Greenport*
White Flower Farmhouse *Southold*

CLOTHING & ACCESSORY SHOPS

Bluestone Lane Beach Collective *Montauk*
Blue & Cream *East Hampton*
Chaser *East Hampton*
Communitie *Bridgehampton*
Clic *East Hampton*
Double RL *East Hampton*
Edward Archer *Southampton*
Joey Wölffer *Sag Harbor*
Katherine Tess *Southampton*
Kirna Zabête *East Hampton*
Marie Eiffel *Shelter Island*
Matriark *Sag Harbor*
Popsicle & Finn *Greenport*
Sabah House *Amagansett*
Satori *Sag Harbor*
Sharis Place *Southampton*
SHOCK *Westhampton Beach*
Surf Bazaar *Montauk*
TENET *Southampton*
Tiina the Store *Amagansett*
The Times Vintage *Greenport*
WAVES *Bridgehampton*

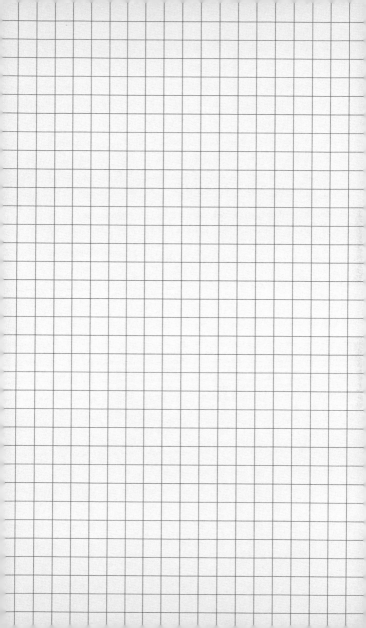

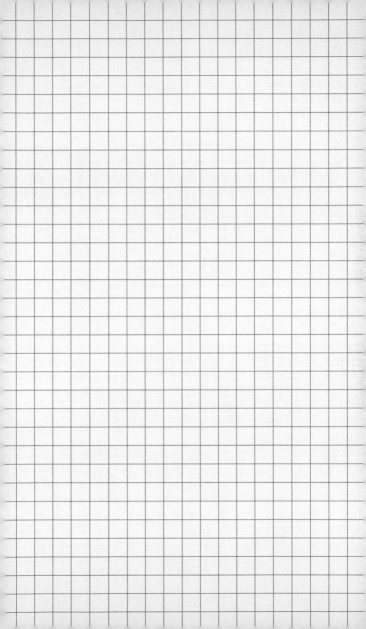

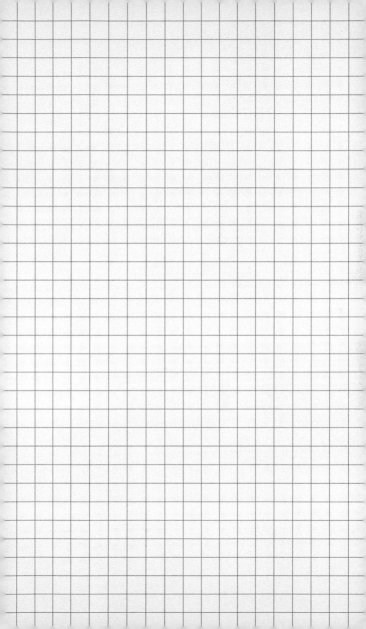

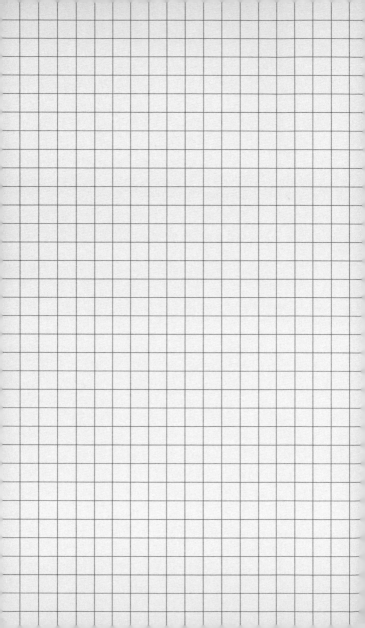

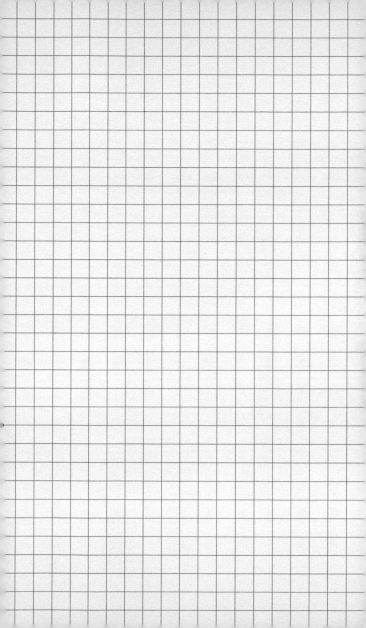